THE ARRIVAL

I Sought God in Hell

by Mietek Weintraub

PENINA PRESS

The Arrival: I Sought God in Hell
Published by Penina Press
Text Copyright © 2012 Mietek Weintraub

COVER DESIGN: Shanie Cooper
EDITOR AND PRODUCTION DIRECTOR: Daniella Barak

Cover image: Women and children on the Birkenau arrival platform known as the "ramp". The Jews were removed from the deportation trains onto the ramp where they faced a selection process- some were sent immediately to their deaths, while others were sent to slave labor. Courtesy of Yad Vashem The Holocaust Martyrs' and Heroes' Remembrance Authority; The Aushwitz Album. The copyright of the photographs from the Auschwitz album (FA-268) are public domain.

Soft Cover ISBN: 978-1-936068-33-3

First edition.

Distributed by:
Urim Publications
POB 52287
Jerusalem 91521, Israel
Tel: 02.679.7633
Fax: 02.679.7634
urim_pub@netvision.net.il

Lambda Publishers, Inc.
527 Empire Blvd.
Brooklyn, NY 11225, USA
Tel: 718.972.5449
Fax: 718.972.6307
mh@ejudaica.com

www.UrimPublications.com

Dedication

To Mama, whose last words to me were:
"Mietek, I'm with the young!"

Contents

Contents

Part I:
The Wheels

Chapter I:
Out of the Ghetto at Last

...staccato, staccato, staccato...

...a clattering, rhythmic rumble...

...wheels of the cattle-car rolling and rattling and clacking, clanging, chugging...

...knocking the steely rails, pounding them, banging them, crushing them...

...hit the track, hit the track, hit the track...

...numbing it, crunching it, smashing it...

...deadening, deadening, deadening...

...staccato, staccato, staccato...

...Lodz-Ghetto, Lodz-Ghetto, Lodz-Ghetto. the ghetto, the ghetto, the ghetto...

The unlit freight train rolls rattling through the dark night, puffing smoke and spurting sparks like some gargantuan black dragon that filled its enormous gut with hundreds of living creatures, and now, sated, crawls hastily and noisily to its cavern to digest its catch in the comfort of familiar surroundings. Soon, it will be ready for the next catch and haul, its abundant prey stacked and stuck in the ghetto as in a cattle corral:

"Whiiiz, Whiiiz!" The dragon hiccups at times with two abrupt, ear-piercing shrieks:

"Whiiiz, Whiiiz!" And hastily it's squirming onward, snorting, spurting and panting.

I try to find some reassurance in the staccato cadence of the wheels beating on the track. There's a kind of stability and tranquility in the monotonously repetitive rhythm. It calms the chaotic thoughts of what is awaiting us. I have never before given the future any thought. Maybe youth is too impatient to wait for the next day. Tomorrow just can't come soon enough, so why even think about it?

And we also have reassurance in the presence of Chaim Rumkowski, our exalted Eldest of the Jews, who is in one of the adjoining cars accompanied by his young bride and also his brother with his wife, though all four of them, most likely, are sitting comfortably in a Pullman and not in an overcrowded cattle car like the rest of us. Among ourselves, we mockingly call him Rumek, or King Chaim the First, to diminish his inflated image with that imposing snow-white mane, thick lips and glasses. With him nearby surely nothing can happen to us…can happen, can happen, can happen…staccato, staccato…

Surely the Germans won't harm their faithful vassal and efficient administrator of the Litzmannstadt Ghetto, who for five harrowing years obediently carried out all their orders for military materiel as well as most of the cruel demands for deportations. This final transport ends the three-month-long liquidation of the ghetto "resettlement", as the Germans call it. We have nothing to fear, they assured us, because they need our labor and various expertise for their war effort, and it would be safer for us to move away from the approaching front…staccato, staccato, staccato…

For days we kept hoping that this final deportation would be called off. We prayed that they'd just leave us alone, but the "evacuation" continued relentlessly and the ghetto was constantly reduced in size, and we had to move to new locations, to live again with total strangers in apartments from which the previous lodgers had already been deported. These last ten weeks of this summer of 1944 were gruesome. We kept begging our Almighty God to perform a miracle so the relentless Germans would just let us be. Like someone condemned to die waits for the verdict to be commuted, we, too, hoped that the transports would stop at the last minute, that a sudden Red Army surge would save us from the unknown and set us free after these five excruciating years of our struggle to survive, battling starvation, disease, shootings, hangings, selections, hoping that our Almighty Merciful God will at last deliver us from this Hitlerite scourge.

It's night. There are subdued sighs, groans, and whimpers in our pitch-black boxcar. We're lying on the floor, densely crammed. If I try to free an arm or a leg from a painful position, those close to me groan and curse. I keep still so as not to disturb Mama lying nearby. She's also quiet and probably concerned about my discomfort. She still dotes over me even though I'm seventeen. And she's always upbeat. Her cheerfulness is my nature too. Her nearness and her constant protection helped sustain me through these last five years of hunger and terror. I can't imagine the world existing without her or myself. And yet, what if the mournful doom-sayers in this car are clairvoyant? Nah, they're just chanting weepers and worriers intensifying the desperate mood on this train ride. The Germans promised we were going to Germany to work, that we wouldn't be separated from our families. They need our labor. The war isn't going well for them. Their own men serve in the army and somebody has to do their civilian work. That's where we come in. Surely the Germans wouldn't get rid of productive laborers while conquering the world… staccato, staccato, staccato…

Chapter 2:
Aunt Hela's Choice

But what if we really are all doomed on this train? What if these are my last moments on this Earth. Shouldn't my life be unreeling now before me. No, no morbid thoughts for me. Mama is with me and that's enough to dispel them. Everything will be fine so long as she's with me. Separated from all my aunts, uncles, and cousins, Mama and I still have each other. Yesterday we parted from Aunt Hela and her husband Sym who defied the German threat that anyone caught in the ghetto after the last transport would be shot on sight. If she and Sym dared to take that gamble, perhaps we should've as well. Mama, now forty-seven, was always close to Hela, her youngest sister, now twenty-seven, whom she protected like a daughter probably because of the twenty-year gap between them. Until Hela married Sym just months before the war, Mama always chaperoned her to dance halls and they went everywhere together.

But yesterday, she left Hela and Sym in their flat to a dangerous and uncertain fate, while she and I went voluntarily to the railroad station to the last transport out of the ghetto. We hope they'll somehow survive because they're in their prime and aren't burdened with small children. Giving birth in the ghetto was strictly forbidden, and once Hela even had to undergo an abortion because of it. All Mama's other sisters and brothers have small children, which are just "useless mouths" to the Hitlerites, who kept collecting and sending them out of the ghetto into the unknown. Luckily, Aunts Asta and Andzia somehow managed to keep their daughters with them to the very end in the ghetto, but were deported a few days before us. Who knows if Hela and Sym made the right decision? Sym surely made the choice to hide and Hela remained with him.

Nine years earlier, her handsome boyfriend Natek Praszkier didn't give her a choice to join him but went to Palestine alone to become a pioneer in a Jewish homeland, leaving Hela heartbroken. She implored him to take her along, but he maintained that she was too delicate for the hardships of a pioneer's life, drying off malaria-infested swamps to make them arable, dwelling in primitive shacks or tents, exposed to scorpions and snakes, fighting off hostile Arab raiders and so on. Natek said that he'd help restore this ancient land lying fallow to its former Biblical glory and make it flow with milk and honey again.

Hela argued that if Poland and Europe weren't safe for Jews anymore, "let us go to America where I have an uncle, Joel Bodzechowski, now Davis, who went there by himself as a teenager in 1899, raised a family and prospered."

Still, Natek reminded her of the Ku-Klux-Klan, the Frank Trial, of hotels and resorts that discriminate against Jews in the USA, and of the Christian Militia of Silver Shirts modeled after Hitler's storm-troopers. And he concluded: "We must find our own land, no matter how small Palestine is, where we have a right to live even though it'll cost us our blood, tears and lives. Only there we can make this claim, for that is our true Land of Israel. Only there our sacrifices will be redeemed. Only there we'll persevere. And only there we'll have the right to bear arms and defend ourselves as Jews in a Jewish land."

"Then I'll go with you," Hela insisted, "and be part of it and build a future for others, and learn how to shoot to defend myself. It'll be easier for us to bear hardships together."

But Natek opposed, claiming that she was too sheltered and pampered for the rigors of the desert: "Maybe someday when we change that arid land into a blooming oasis, turn the sands into arable soil and plant forests and orchards, you too will come there. But the rugged life and the scorching sun will soon parch your delicate features and turn your skin to wrinkles. Your dad would much rather find someone wealthy for you who's settled right here in Lodz. He'd be very hurt if you left him now that his wife is dying of cancer."

Hela was heartsick after Natek had left Poland. Soon he sent her some snapshots from Palestine. He was out on some rocky terrain in the company of a few other young men, some in helmets, all in khaki shorts, some holding spades, others rifles. All were tan and cheerful. I cherished these few photos – I was fascinated by the rifles – and looked at them probably more often than my pining Aunt Hela did. Eventually, I put them in my own album and Aunt Hela never asked for them after she had married Sym three years later. Even now they're in my knapsack with my other cherished things.

Mama tried to console Aunt Hela about Natek's emigration, explaining that he couldn't cope with the pressure of facing responsibility; that, instead, he took the easy way out by trying to impress everyone with his daring and manliness; that, instead of returning his parents' love by finding a job, marrying Hela and rewarding them with beautiful grandchildren, he, like a coward, evaded these obligations and took off for an uncertain future in a barren, hostile land. Aunt Hela was inconsolable and pined after Natek for a long time. Mama took Hela to dances to help her find a new man, but Hela kept comparing her new acquaintances to her beloved Natek, all unfavorably, until she met Sym.

Chapter 3:
Decisions

We had little choice in making decisions during the last five years. Once the Germans defined us as Jews, we had to follow their ever-more-restrictive ordinances. In the first months, some daredevils who didn't "look Jewish" got into lines for bread that were off-limits to Jews. But they risked denunciation by Polish acquaintances and then a beating by German soldiers. Those who looked Aryan and could afford "Aryan papers" paid small fortunes for baptismal certificates, then moved to another city to evade recognition by Polish acquaintances. Theirs was a very risky decision; they also had to join a Catholic Church, drop any traces of Jewish intonation while speaking Polish, and stop all contacts with their Jewish relatives remaining in the ghetto. Simply – erase their past.

Aunt Hela and Sym decided not to "go Aryan" then, but to share the lot of all Jews – a bad decision in view of the draconian measures the Germans soon unleashed on us. Once they herded us into a ghetto, cutting us off from any contact with the Poles, it was too late to run or to buy false birth certificates. Baluty, the slum section of Lodz, was cordoned off as a ghetto. The Germans launched a campaign of terror to prompt us into abandoning our pre-war homes and moving into the squalid ghetto, which they sealed off at the end of April 1940 with 180,000 Jews. To justify such an outrageous and antiquated decree as quarantining Jews, the Germans depicted us as bearers of contagious diseases, criminals, unproductive and unwilling to do honest work. To keep the Poles neutral, or even to curry favor with them, Hitler tried to pass himself off as their deliverer from Jewish infestation and his conquest of Poland as his mission – a Christian crusade.

Our in-laws, the Brodt family, were the only ones who dared to go Aryan. Lonia Brodt, her son Semek, who was my age, and daughter Hela, all had blond hair and pug noses, and wouldn't arouse the slightest suspicion by trying to pass themselves off as Aryans. Lonia was the sister of Uncle Henryk Wolborski who married Mama's sister, Asta. Hela Brodt was a close friend of Aunt Hela; both shared the same age and even looks. But their contact had to stop so as not to endanger the Brodt's cover on the Aryan side.

The decision to run was another option. Before our ghetto was girded with barbed wire and guarded by sentries, Great Aunt Rozia Maliniak nee Bodzechowski took that desperate chance with her husband Aaron twice but failed. Before the war, Aaron was a merchant in timber and a partner in the huge Maliniak Lumber Yard on Gdanska Street and could even afford to send his older son, Julek, to study abroad. He surely must have had timber-trade acquaintances among rural Poles with whom he and Rozia could possibly find shelter, either for a price or for their good will. But it was very risky. Even if he succeeded in escaping from the ghetto, living with Poles presented its own dangers as their neighbors could report them for harboring Jews. Aaron probably managed to rescue some valuables with which to bribe whomever he could when making his way out of the ghetto, or maybe even to make his way out of Poland. But his two attempts failed, and he was brought back and probably much poorer. The third time Aaron decided to leave Aunt Rozia with us and break out by himself. Soon she had a nightmare that he got shot in the head. We never heard from him again.

The third decision was the one on which we had resolved three days ago: hiding! Still it was very risky. First, we had no food or hope of finding any in the nearly empty ghetto, and we were very, very hungry. Second, disregarding German orders to show up for deportation was very dangerous: if discovered, we could be shot on the spot. And yet we still tried hiding. Sym even dared to bribe an SS man who clomped up the stairs with his rifle at the ready. If he reached our flat, he'd find us crouching on the floor and shaking in fear. But Sym approached the soldier one flight below and gave him some valuables. The SS man left, surely laughing that we wouldn't evade capture anyway, while he, meanwhile, got richer. Thanks to Uncle Sym's daring and the wealthy Uncle Heniek's valuables, (Uncle Heniek was also hiding with us with Aunt Asta and little Lilka), we won another day of staying together and drawing comfort from each other's presence.

To lure us out of hiding, the Germans promised bread and marmalade to anyone who showed up for the final transport, and they assured us that Rumkowski would also share our ride out of the ghetto. In earlier years, when they needed workers outside the ghetto and enticed us with promises of more food and decent living conditions, volunteers were reluctant to go because they didn't trust deceptive Nazi promises, which kept us forever off balance and making the wrong decisions. But in the company of our King, they surely wouldn't try to deceive us!

Still, our decision to go voluntarily was marred by a bad omen: Mama shattered a mirror while packing last night. She stood over the splinters mortified with foreboding. I was sickened with grief, watching her, but with the threat of getting shot outright, what could I say to cheer her? What choice did we really have?

Chapter 4:
The Comfortable Cousins

Besides leaving behind lovely Aunt Hela with her husband Sym, we also parted from the uppity Aunt Asta with her artful husband Heniek Wolborski and their cute younger daughter, the twelve-year-old Lilka. Their older daughter, Stefa, now eighteen, was shipped out of the ghetto earlier with other hospital patients where she was laid out with the flu, or something; at least that's what I was told, though now I think leaving her there with only a flu was extremely risky. Germans had no use for sick Jews.

Stefa at eighteen was a full-fledged woman and, unlike me, surely had a lot of romantic experience. She was a tall, shapely, attractive brunette, with wavy hair and big eyes, and was very mature. In the ghetto, she was a policewoman for a while, a rather fortunate position rewarded with extra food rations. To land this kind of a plum, a girl had to be a high school graduate with a diploma from the ghetto and have plenty of *protektzia* (clout), which Uncle Heniek surely must have had. The female police service began at the end of '42, and Stefa joined it in '43 when she turned eighteen. These young women were good-looking and smartly dressed in green uniforms, short trousers, short waistless jackets, and round caps. On one arm, they bore the insignia of the Order Service and carried nightsticks, which they probably never had to use. It was never clear for what service the Order was kept. But with their young, feminine figures strolling in pairs through the drab ghetto streets, they were a welcome sight anyway. I was proud that one of these pretty girls was my own cousin Stefa. But my pride was short-lived when, in March of 1943, the Order was disbanded. So long as it lasted, Stefa was walking proud in her chic uniform, which also gave her ample exposure to the most eligible young men. Surely she lived life to the fullest, enjoying her moments with handsome boyfriends.

Like Stefa, Lilka, too, had a very cheerful personality and an open face enhanced by her button snub-nose, a cute narrow groove on her upper lip, and a full mouth slightly pouting. Her narrowed, ever-smiling, and slightly mischievous eyes were set above her still nicely rounded cheeks, while all the other ghetto faces were gaunt. Ghetto grief didn't frazzle her spontaneous nature or erode her innate cheerfulness. She played a lot and laughed often in her carefree way, with a lust for life and the relish of a good time. Her straight dark hair, cut in a stylish page-boy fashion, added to her girlish glow. Surely because of her father's connections, she survived the dreadful Selection two years ago when all children under ten were forcibly taken from their parents and shipped out.

For Stefa and Lilka, the ghetto years were not as traumatic as for me, Mama and Dad, who were starving. Their father Heniek Wolborski knew some important people and a few days ago told us confidentially that we were headed for a place called Auschwitz, but nothing else.

Before the war Heniek had a flourishing business, distributing fabrics on the busy Piotrkowska Street. When the Germans started their persecutions of Jews, Heniek, like his sister Lonia Brodt, could surely afford to buy some Aryan papers for his family before being herded into the ghetto. But with his Semitic looks, he chanced exposure. So he moved into the ghetto with the rest of us where he even managed to land some administrative position so that his wife and girls were never too hungry. And now, after all these years, the artful Uncle Heniek, too, must give up his relative stability to an uncertain future with Aunt Asta and little Lilka. But would his wheeling and dealing help him to keep his family provided for and out of harm's way wherever we were going now?

Chapter 5:
Into the Unknown

...the ghetto, the ghetto, the ghetto...

...away from its confining barbed wires...

T he cattle-cars seemed endless when Mama and I got on yesterday with thousands of others. When they shut the latch, we instantly felt deceived and trapped because the Germans reneged on their promise to give bread and marmalade to everyone who'd appear voluntarily. This was cruel, for we haven't eaten in days since the cooperatives were shut and their staffs deported. And now, having left Aunts Hela and Asta with their families, we are alone crammed with these strangers. We're starved and worried. Are we indeed on our way to work in Germany? Surely the Germans wouldn't deprive themselves of all our valuable handiwork, and they'll put our skills to use again. Haven't we proved ourselves in these five years as artisans, mechanics, and technicians? We've been practically self-sustaining as we turned out German military uniforms, caps, furs, gloves, boots, carpets, munitions, nails, and electrical equipment so vital for their war economy. In one week, seventy-five thousand workers in ninety enterprises produced uniforms for five-thousand soldiers and filled out orders for the German army, navy, and air force.

A whole new cadre of skilled workers grew up during these last five years – teenagers who, like me, learned a trade to become valuable to the Germans and avoid deportation. I've become an electrician – well, I started to. I haven't done many functional things yet, but I know a lot of theory, and with some more schooling, I would be on my way to becoming an electrical engineer. Before being deported, I was still a drudge, scraping the charred enamel coating off the copper wire and attending vocational classes on the second floor of the plant.

High-ranking SS officers, Gestapo officials and, once, even Himmler visited the ghetto shops to inspect production. They were amazed at the quality and quantity of our work each time. They probably wondered if these were the same Jews portrayed by their propaganda as vile parasitic leeches, living off Christian labor. Surely they wouldn't want to harm their economy now by hurting us. We even tried to trust them when they said: "You must get away from the Russians who'll punish you for aiding our war effort." Hans Biebow, the German Ghetto Chief, promised to send us all into Germany, "where you'll be safe from air raids and the approaching Russian front, and where you'll continue working in your trades in peace and security." Now there is a switch: the Russians intend to harm us while the Germans try to protect us. Surely he was mocking, but all we could do was to pretend that we believed in his good intentions. The Germans used the same deceptive logic five years ago when they, at first, tried to lure us INTO the ghetto: "It's for your own protection from the local population who hate you anyway," they claimed then, assuring us that we'd be safer by ourselves and away from the Polish Christians.

Yet when we asked Biebow for more food in the days of famine, he said: "How can you Jews expect a good treatment from us Germans while the American planes are bombing our homeland, leveling our homes, and killing our women and children?" That was his Hitlerite logic: to take it out on us, defenseless and starved in Poland, because bombs were falling on Germany in a war that Hitler started with the West. We were in no position to question such reasoning while being in the wolf's fangs. We were surrounded tightly by trigger-happy sentries, and continuously admonished by our King Rumek to keep our noses close to the grindstone and not cause any trouble.

And now we lie in this cattle-car, mulling over Biebow's reassuring last speeches: "Take your workbenches with you. We, the German People, know how to appreciate Jewish workmanship. Come by the trainload. Report voluntarily! Take your pots and pans! You'll need them in Germany." And he added that the machinery from ghetto shops was being shipped to Germany, too, so that our workers could continue production for the German war effort in a safer place inside Germany. He assured us with his "personal word of honor" that everything would be reassembled for production in Germany and that even our Eldest of the Jews was traveling with us as proof of our orderly transfer. Even Dr. Bradfisch, the Gestapo Chief of Litzmannstadt, addressed us with a lulling "You are on a voyage to an easier future," while their army was strategically retreating. We would like to believe it, but because of German duplicity, it leaves nagging doubts. Who knows? We will soon find out.

There are rumors in the car about a concentration camp, a horrible place, though no one has ever been there, and no one knows for sure. Some women are mournfully chanting: "Ah, me, woe is me! An end, a bitter end has descended upon us." Others are consoling them: "Our Almighty will provide for us. He'll watch over us. He won't let us perish." But the lamenters are inconsolable: "Why, Dear Lord, hast Thou forsaken us? Have mercy on your Children of Israel, Almighty Ruler of Heavens!"

But our prayers and oaths have flowed for five years and our lot has been worsening, while Hitler, with all the curses on him, perseveres. We've been beseeching God to prove His existence as in Biblical times. If He stayed Abraham's axe just in time from slaying his son, why can't He do it now when *all* His sons may be on the executioner's block?

Chapter 6:
Magic Wheels

...staccato, staccato, staccato...

...the beating, the pounding, the throbbing...

...go forwards, to progress, to progress...

And yet with all the physical discomfort, grim circumstances, and these ever nagging hunger pains, I find this train ride engrossing. It's been five years since I last sat on a train or any other kind of moving vehicle. And train rides have always stirred my excitement of anticipated adventure a la Jack London's carefree drifter.

Ah, the thrill of riding on wheels! Even horse-driven droshkies or drays drew me with their clopping hubble-bubble on the cobblestones of pre-war Lodz. Once, when I was eleven, I hopped on the rear of a moving droshky by imitating Cesiek, our tenement janitor's son, for whom this was a favorite foolhardiness – getting a free ride, then jumping off in heavy traffic and making a dash for the sidewalk. The wily cabbie horsewhipped me, but I bore the burning pain across my back all for the thrill of riding those magical wheels. If my parents or Grandpa found out about my foolhardiness, they'd have been dismayed that their well-behaved momma's boy acted like a ruffian, putting himself in harm's way. But in hindsight, this pre-war folly had been minor. During the last five years, one would endanger one's life just by walking within a German sentry's shooting range. By then, the social order of the Jewish middle-class had almost crumbled. Parents lost control. Just trying to stay alive was a daring feat.

Trains used to transport me on vacation out of the sooty city of Lodz, the "Polish Manchester," and into green nature. The train ride was always a prelude to fun and leisure. My imagination used to transform the scenery of the refreshing countryside into the wilderness of James Fenimore Cooper, Zane Gray, or Karol May. Traps, hostility and danger were lurking everywhere; the rumbling train wheels – an intense beat of Indian war drums, with the Indians galloping alongside the train on horseback waving tomahawks and shouting ferociously. But what chance did a bunch of half-clad braves have against the iron monster, advancing with detested colonists? Hitler, too, in his youth, read the popular German author Karl May's Indian stories. I wonder if he saw them as alien minorities fit only for abuse, and expulsion to reservations, or as undaunted underdogs trying to resist the oppressive invaders.

Now we're in a cattle car, with only one small, barred hole way up near the ceiling. It's dark already. People are twisted on the floor. Those in need to relieve themselves make their way to the huge vat near the door by stumbling over the others who groan and curse them. I'm too shy and won't use that vat in the presence of so many people, even in the darkness. I also worry that I'd miss it and pee over those lying right next to it. Mama probably has to go too, because traumatic events cause her stomach pains and diarrhea. Yet, she, too, isn't moving from her spot on the floor next to me. I try to block out the gruesome noises inside by focusing on the magic rhythm of clattering wheels so calming in its monotony. I think of the flourishing August landscape outside that we haven't seen in five years, with stretches of farmland ready for harvest, the fragrance of fresh hay, clover, honeysuckle, mint, chamomile…anything to neutralize the stench from the huge vat that serves the needs of some hundred people in here.

This train ride ends five years of confinement in the squalid ghetto, while I'm availing myself of distance and of speed through modern technology, civilization's means to a brighter future. The clattering wheels are now the clippety-clop of a steed which will soar with me over the dark clouds. The rhythmic, repetitive, hypnotic beat has a calming effect – everything is under control; exciting things await us at our destination.

The last time I was on wheels was years ago when I pedaled a bike to deliver bills for the Ghetto Tischlerei (Ghetto Joiner's Workshop), which supplied ghetto factories with stools, tables and cabinets. I rode it for five months before it was taken from me. A fourteen-year-old kid on a bike in a ghetto, where all adults were stripped of any conveniences of mechanized locomotion, was much too conspicuous anyway. And it always caused envious glances cast at me and the bike. So I had to deliver the bills on foot. I didn't grieve the loss of the bike for long because Master-Foreman Fuchs, who took it away from me, had to surrender it as well. The German ghetto administrators were not making life in the least bit easier for any Jew. Modern conveniences such as wheels, whether pedaled or pulled by animals or run on motors, became off-limits to us – with the sole exception of King Chaim who had at his disposal a horse-driven droshky with a beefy coachman, Eisenman. Now, the Hitlerites are accommodating Jews with a free train ride of all things – that's the more reason to enjoy this miserable ride.

Wheels became a privilege reserved only for Germans. One would think they invented the wheel from the way they denied it to the Jews. Perhaps the impressive motorization of their army and their exaltation of wheels symbolize to them a road to victory as stated by the slogan posted on every military train: "*Raeder musten rollen fur den Sieg* (Wheels must roll for victory)." With a mighty roar of motors, they triumphantly rolled into Lodz in the second week of September 1939. Hundreds of motorcycles emerged suddenly, swarming busily to and fro on our main commercial thoroughfare, Piotrkowska Street. Each had a side car in which sat a soldier in a steel helmet, green raincoat and field glasses hanging from his neck, and each held an automatic gun. The drivers were clad likewise, with a rifle across their back. They looked like some prowling robot invaders, an illusion that was enhanced by the roar of engines saturating the air with a strange new odor of gasoline and billowing exhaust fumes.

Busily the motorcycles kept flanking the marching soldiers, thousands of them in massive steel helmets with faces exuding self-assurance, arrogance and a singleness of purpose. Soldiers marched in parade fashion to the roll of drums, slamming the pavement with their hobnail boots like a mammoth sledge hammer trying to crush it. Slam! Bam! Each bam, each slam, was a hobnail driven into the coffin of our happy bygone days with the gigantic swastika wheel rounded off at the edges, giving it the semblance of a wheel of progress. Or was it ominously suspended over us as it was about to turn and grind us under it?

Chapter 7:
Prostrate Lodz

In the frantic days preceding the war, Polish ultra-nationalistic songs were blasting from loudspeakers all day: "The sea, the sea, our sea." These were enhanced by patriotic slogans: "We're strong, tight-ranked and prepared," and, in response to Hitler's demands for a corridor to Danzig: "We won't give up even one button." When the war started, a new sound enveloped Lodz – the shrill and mournful wailing of air raid sirens and loud-speakers blasting cryptic messages: "Attention, attention. It's coming," followed by letters and numbers that were probably codes for military intelligence.

During air raids, we would run down for cover in entrance gates of tenements, though we knew that they didn't offer any protection from bombs. But Lodz was spared from any destruction probably because it didn't offer any visible resistance. One bomb that fell on Lodz I remember with dismay. We stood trembling in the gateway of our tenement at 72 Wolczanska Street, when we heard the sinister drone of the bomber formations overhead, followed by heavy reports but didn't know then the difference between flak and bomb blasts. At once we learned. A thunderous detonation, several streets away, shook our house to its foundation. A deadly hush fell upon us. This, then, was the sound of war!

"My factory! They hit my factory! The bomb fell on my plant!" Grandpa exclaimed. We found out later that his premonition was partly right: the bomb leveled a ten-story apartment house just across the alley from Grandpa's plant at its new location at 2 Zamenhofa Street, where he moved it just a month earlier. His textile mill was damaged on the outside but remained operable, while the ten-story tenement across the alley collapsed, killing its trapped tenants, who, like most of us, didn't even have any shelters to hide in. Was Grandpa psychic or was he just an instinctive worrier, I wonder.

That bomb crushed our previous gaiety just like the tenement with its dwellers. Only a week earlier Lodz was still reverberating with music and cheer. "Sweet Georgia Brown," a hit from the USA, was sung to Polish lyrics. So was a trendy dance the "Lambeth Walk". American jazz was the latest craze. And beneath all this exuberance was a fatalistic resignation that whatever will happen, will happen.

And then Hitler attacked. Grandpa and my uncles knew it was coming. They knew Hitler was itching for conflict and that he had it in for the Jews, but where could they run? How could they shut down their businesses and factories and set out with women and children into strange lands as homeless refugees? At least in Lodz they had their good name and status in the community. On the road through foreign lands they'd neither be able to communicate nor provide food and shelter for their wives and little children.

After Hitler invaded Poland, there was still a chance to run for a week or so. Some Jews fled by boat, others on anything with wheels. There were even those who made their way on foot over the border to Romania or the Soviet Union. But those who had small children or who were frail or old stayed, hoping that the Germans would remain civilized enough to treat them decently and humanely. Most Jews didn't even try to flee; they reasoned that because Poland had a pact with France and England, those two mighty western powers "would crush Hitler in one blow." In vain we watched the blue skies searching for their aircraft. None came. Only German planes, with total impunity, ruled the Polish sky over prostrate Lodz. Poland's two allies never interfered with Hitler's rape of our city or the rest of Poland. Our helplessness was humiliating.

Chapter 8:
The Nightmare Begins

T he restraints against the Jews of Lodz came a month after Hitler's army had conquered the rest of Poland. Its ally, the Red Army, moved into Eastern Poland. Due to the initial absence of anti-Jewish hostilities, many Jews, who at first managed to get over to the Russian side, returned to their homes in German-occupied Poland. Many still had respect for German culture and fairness. But these Germans were of a different breed and not the usually tolerant soldiers from World War I. Even their marching songs projected hostility and aggression as they paraded through our city.

Wir wollen weiter marchieren	[We want to keep on marching
Wen alles in Scherben faellt	Till all will fall to bits,
Denn heute gehoert uns Deutschland	Today we lord o'er Deutschland
Und morgen die ganze Welt	Tomorrow we'll own the world.][1]

And the huge, cheering crowds of excited German-talking, flower-tossing, and flag-waving *Volksdeutsche* (Ethnic Germans living outside the Third Reich), many with swastika bands on their arms and banners, welcomed the conquering troops by screaming joyously and hailing them with the Nazi salute. Apprehensively, we watched the alien soldiers from behind drawn curtains in Aunt Asta's apartment on the main street, where we moved in temporarily with Grandpa and Aunt Helen for the security of being in the public eye in the center of town. Uncle Sym and thousands of

---

1   Author's translation

able-bodied young men had fled the city before the advancing Germans. But why did we, women, children and the elderly, have to stay out of sight? Just a few days ago, there was some talk on how highly civilized and rational the Germans were, and how their advanced technology and culture would benefit the mostly rural Poland. Mama, ever so cheerful, even tried to make light of it by joking that we'd be saving money on a jaunt to Germany since Lodz was now a part of it. The adults explained to me that it was safer to keep off the street because whenever the local populace was unhappy for any reason, the Jews always provided a convenient outlet for their frustration. My family hoped that even the Hitlerites wouldn't commit any brazen acts on our busy main street, and thus, decided to brave the storm at the Wolborskis' place in midtown.

But Mama's attempts at humor were marred by the mobs of elated Volksdeutsche, their frenzied faces contorted with hate and power, their stiffly raised arms piercing the air like a forest of bayonets, their hysterical shrieks: "*Sieg heil! Sieg heil!* (To victory! To glory!)". We were stunned and dismayed by a sudden spate of swastika banners on our main street and by the eruption of so many civilians in our city who rejoiced at the German military presence, and by their disciplined display of seething aggressiveness.

"*Huete ab!* (Hats off!)" barked a civilian with a swastika band on his arm to a spectator, and, before the stunned man could even react, the civilian Nazi knocked his hat off with a vigorous slap to the head that sent the onlooker reeling. Only the dense crowd of parade watchers cushioned the man from tumbling to the pavement.

The entering troops were a spectacle of power so overwhelming as if to convince the spectators that nothing in the world could challenge German might. Their boots crushing the pavement in pompous unison, the solemn drum roll, the deafening roar of their thousands of motors, and the sudden upsurge of ecstatic crowds, roaring their ear-splitting "*Sieg heil!*" were reverberating like Wagner's "Ride of the Valkyrie".

We thought of it all as the ecstasy of victory but didn't feel directly threatened by the victors so long as Jews were not singled out for abuse. We assumed that we'd be treated like a conquered people but no worse than our Polish Christian compatriots. It was a deceptive calm before a deadly storm.

There was some violence but we minimized it as isolated incidents and not as German policy. The first one we witnessed two days after their victory came when we were still holed up in the Wolborskis' apartment. Two stout, middle-age soldiers came into the vast tenement at 37 Piotrkowska Street, and, claiming to be despondent over their comrades who fell in the battle for Poland, demanded a tribute in cash and valuables from all Jewish tenants or else they'd ransack every apartment and shoot some of us in the process. Since the Jews had started this war, according to Hitler, they said, that made us all guilty of their comrades' deaths. I watched from Aunt Asta's flat how the few terrified Jews, whom these bandits grabbed and delegated to do the extortion, scurried through all the apartments in the vast complex collecting the ransom from equally mortified tenants. They then dutifully delivered it to the two "grief-stricken" warriors who were standing in the center of the huge courtyard with pistols in their hands. We were scared and so outraged that some of the robbed Jews even thought of going to the military headquarters to lodge a complaint.

Chapter 9:
The Stranglehold Tightens

In retrospect, it was ridiculous for Jews to expect the German military headquarters to take disciplinary action against those two soldiers who robbed a whole tenement of Jews at gunpoint! Our thinking then only reflects the high esteem that Polish Jews still held for German fairness. But that esteem was quickly evaporating.

A couple of days after the Germans occupied Lodz, they plundered Uncle Sewek's motorcycles and bicycles store in an upscale section of our city at 72 Piotrkowska Street while I was there visiting. A German army officer requisitioned everything in the store, and when Uncle Sewek asked for a receipt, the officer scribbled something on a scrap of paper and handed it to him. But there was no way to collect on it. It was just a worthless slip of paper that the Germans had surely no intention to honor because they regarded any Jewish property as obtained dishonestly by Jews in the first place.

That looting affected me personally because I had hopes for a bike as a gift for my upcoming bar mitzvah from Uncle Sewek and Aunt Renia, Mama's second younger sister. Renia, who married Sewek Opatowski, was with him in the store, too, helping out as usual. She was always very warm to Mama and ever ready to help out her less prosperous sister. I always liked to visit them at their busy store with its distinctive smell of rubber tires. I was glad to have an uncle with that kind of a business. One summer before the war, he even took me along to see a bike race in which he promoted his tires and bikes. We rode in a taxi down the racing route, anxiously watching the progress of the contender on Uncle Sewek's bike. To our disappointment his biker lost that race.

Soon, all Jews had to surrender their bikes, motorcycles, cars, radios and furs, and then were dispossessed of their businesses and factories. And in a few weeks, we were kicked out of our homes to make room for ethnic Germans who joined the Nazi Party.

We soon learned how civilized and rational the Nazis really were. Despite their lightning-speed conquest of Poland, they blamed us for their negligible losses in life because Hitler told them that "If war broke out, Jews would be responsible for it."

Some Jews queried "But why us?"

"Because we are the most vulnerable," others replied.

Suddenly we felt very, very vulnerable. There we were, fair game to any German who decided to take it out on us. It was a bad omen. And, sure enough, it was repeated over and over throughout those five dreadful years.

The Germans were always sore and angry – we were blamed for their bad moods.

The Germans were always self-righteous – we were always the culprits.

The Germans felt always slighted – we were always the offenders.

They were chaste and pure – we were always a festering sore.

They were always just and fair – we were always the scheming perpetrators.

They were the exalted liberators of Europe – we were the scourge of the Earth to be cleansed by them. Jew, Jude, or Zhid – all these German and Polish words now became a curse and an affliction, a dreaded signal for us to run, and for them to give chase. They uttered them with such revulsion as if we were the carriers of a rampaging plague.

The streets of Lodz looked alien, deserted. They lost their former lively hustle and bustle. They were no longer filled with people, or children, or horse-drawn lorries and droshkies. Gone were the many mouth-watering aromas. There were no mothers pushing or rocking their strollers in parks or on the sunny boulevards. It wasn't even called Lodz anymore; the Germans incorporated it into the Reich as Litzmannstadt, named in honor of their general who conquered it in World War I. They also evacuated and resettled local Poles to make room for incoming Germans. Lodz suddenly lost its former character.

A hush fell over the once bubbling metropolis. Only military vehicles, mostly trucks with confiscated Jewish property, were noisily crossing the hushed streets. The avenues and boulevards were now studded with German soldiers strolling leisurely and self-assuredly, viewing everything with a superior and bored familiarity while smoking their German cigarettes. Jews were soon prohibited from riding streetcars, driving cars, or attending movies, theaters, concerts, museums, parks, zoos and just about anything that could bring us enjoyment. To show our respect for the "Master Race", a Jew had to doff his hat before any German in uniform and quickly step off the sidewalk and walk on the road lest he contaminate the soldier with his very nearness. Jews stayed home for fear of getting caught "for work," which usually meant loading or unloading military trucks with confiscated goods from Jewish stores and warehouses. In the course of a few weeks, the prosperous merchants and manufacturers of Lodz faced financial ruin and, stripped of all rights, became indigent. The Poles were not bothered, and Polish girls often strolled on the boulevards attracting appreciative comments from the ambling German soldiers who seemed to have finally found something in Lodz worth relishing.

German degradations of Jews grew with each day. Even though we experienced excesses from Polish hooligans before the war, this abuse was so unprecedented that our whole world suddenly became very bleak. German soldiers, as if not having a worry in the world, would stop orthodox Jews on the street and meticulously shear off their beards, all to the great amusement of gentile passers-by. Jews were also caught on the street, dragged out of their homes and subjected to humiliating and exhaustive labor, cleaning streets or public toilets, or forced to do physical work while being jeered and brutalized. It didn't matter that these Jews were on their way to a hospital, or to a doctor, or had other urgent business; to the German soldiers, we were all fair game.

Cruelty and brutality took over compassion for human pain and misery. The civilized world of Central Europe was regressing to the Dark Ages. If a Jew dared to venture out of his home and into the street, it was only on a most urgent need. Quickly, surreptitiously, as if trying to be invisible, slinking through side-streets, alleys, and by-ways and scurrying along the walls like mice, we tried to reach our destination without attracting attention. It was easy to spot a Jew walking: hunched, head down, a hasty, nervous gait, and always in a great hurry – all of which was in such stark contrast with the relaxed saunter of the German soldiers and the strutting of the Volksdeutsche (German ethnics) who carried on as if they themselves had conquered Lodz from the Poles.

We were gripped by a constrained feeling of impending doom. We were experiencing a sinister atmosphere, a foreboding intangible fear, an apocalyptic kind of catastrophe hovering over us, a nagging feeling of strangulation in the constrictive coils of a serpent. To try and leave our town for another locality was very risky because of sentries at every check-post who often shot straying Jews. Hoping for safety in numbers, most Jews remained in Lodz where our population, due to forced resettlements from other areas, had swelled to two-hundred thousand.

After several months, we were forced to wear yellow armbands on our left arm that defined us as Jews. We were rapidly losing any sense of self-worth and began to feel like pariahs. And we were frightened. Yet there were some daredevils among us who defied the order to display their yellow armbands because they did not "look Jewish" and spoke fluent, unaccented Polish. But even they were easily spotted by a tormented look in their hounded eyes, or just by the way they walked. Our beloved Lodz turned into a cage for us, with the Germans regarding us, with our yellow armbands, like some bizarre lepers who must not be tolerated nor remain in their new, purified society.

It was hard for me to believe that just a few weeks earlier my family praised the German culture and humanism, preferring Germans to uncivilized Russians as occupiers. Germans were still remembered from World War I as accommodating and courteous while Russians were branded as savage Cossacks. Both Berlin and Vienna were regarded as centers of law, order and culture. Jews esteemed the jovial Germans and adopted their work ethic, thriftiness, and even a part of their old German language some centuries ago, which became spoken Yiddish for them and flourished in literature and on the stage.

That was the thinking then, five years ago. Who would have suspected that the Austrians and Germans with their gay waltzes and weepy sentimentality would turn out to be such barbarians? And yet, now that our ghetto has been liquidated and we are off to somewhere, we still hope to be spared from doom so long as we can perform useful work in carpentry, metal-working, uniform-sewing, or even simple manual labor like digging ditches. After all, the Germans are practical people and wouldn't waste all this potential labor resource.

Chapter 10:
The Nazi Crusaders

Wir fahren nach Polen   [To Poland we are jogging
Um Juden zu versohlen   To give the Jews a flogging.][1]

This slogan, scrawled in chalk on military trains and trucks that rolled into Poland with the invading troops seemed as if the soldiers in these vehicles had written it for fun; as if their subjugation of another nation was just a big joke. Nazi propaganda minimized their war simply as a campaign "to settle accounts with the Jews" and liberate the Poles from the "Jewish bacillus" as if saying: "You see, Polish people, we have nothing against you personally. We'll just help you clean your house of the Jewish pestilence."

Did the natives accept Hitler's message? Many see Jews as Christ killers. The Catholic Church had been broadcasting this for centuries. Surely many Poles thought that the Jews had it coming to them. Aside from their fervent Catholicism, some Poles were ultra-nationalistic and wanted Poland cleared of all minorities anyway, regarding all Jews, even the most assimilated ones, as aliens.

The public abuse of Jews, often to the merriment of some Polish onlookers, sent a message to Poles that they, as brothers in Christianity, were not a target of German grievance. To enhance this feeling, the Nazis freed the Poles from employment in Jewish businesses and households and even rewarded them for reporting hidden Jews. The Poles were also

---

1   Author's translation

left in relative control of their lives and could move freely around Lodz, strolling down the boulevards, visiting parks, zoos, and allowed in movies and theaters.

And the Brave Crusaders/Knights of the Broken Cross also liberated domestic animals from "Jewish domination." We wondered: Was it also to release them from "Jewish domination" or just to deprive Jews of the calming company of pets?

Aunt Hela got a young German shepherd dog, Lord, some weeks before the war. She and Uncle Sym were just married and probably wanted to delay having children in those uncertain times of the Hitler menace. I loved playing with Lord whenever I visited them. He was friendly, playful and well-behaved. When he once got sick, Aunt Hela was inconsolable. Her eyes would well up with tears as she kept patting and kissing him on the head and cooing: "Nice doggy, good Lordie." When he recovered, Aunt Hela was overjoyed. When the Germans soon ordered Jews to surrender all pets "for adoption by non-Jews," there were rumors that they were really killing them all. I never tried to find out what Aunt Hela did with Lord, hoping that she and Uncle Sym found a nice Polish family who adopted him. Why would anyone destroy a faithful animal that could offer so much warmth and even give up its life to protect its owner?

The pets disappeared from the streets, which were now flooded with swastikas. Like the Christian cross, it reminded Jews that it wasn't our symbol, that we didn't belong here, and we had no right to rejoice in seeing them. This new twisted black cross emblazoned in a white circle on a red flag was not so much a symbol of someone's creed as it was an emblem of exclusion, taunting us with its menacing omnipresence. You and yours wouldn't accept me, so suffer, the cross seemed to be saying. But the swastika grinned at us with its contorted grimace: You couldn't accept me even if you wanted to because you're unfit and unwelcome, so don't even come near. Just cringe before me!

Chapter 11:
A Walk Through the Park

Soon after the German conquest of Lodz, I was on an errand near the Sienkiewicz Park where, for years, I spent many hours playing with my friend Walek Axelrod, who lived nearby. If I took a short cut through it, I could save a lot of time. But parks, among other places, were now off limits to Jews. I was also curious how the park looked and to see if any of my former playmates were still there having a good time, or simply to capture some happy memories. If I just passed it quickly and in a purposeful way, without even stopping, no one would bother me. I also didn't notice anyone guarding the gate. And I don't look Jewish enough to attract anyone's attention.

I entered through the iron gate and walked briskly without even looking around. The park was almost empty except for a few isolated elderly people resting on benches. Some German soldiers were strolling in the company of giggling young women. Absent were the dozens of happy children, running, shouting and laughing who filled the park just weeks ago. Nowhere to be seen were the bevies of mothers on benches, rocking their baby buggies. It seemed eerily quiet, depressing and desolate for a place this lovely. I imagined a cemetery looking somewhat like this.

Halfway through the park and stepping perhaps a little too briskly for someone on a stroll, I sensed that I was being watched. I quickened my pace even more when a figure darted toward me. I was soon overtaken and stopped by a tall boy with straight blond hair in a khaki shirt and short pants with a swastika armband and a whip in his hand. I recognized Klaus who sometimes used to play ball with us. I might have even heard his last name Kinski or something, surely an ethnic German, now in Hitler Youth uniform.

"You are Jude, aren't you?" he gasped in Polish but using the German word for Jew.

I nodded.

"What?! I don't hear you," he snapped furiously and close to my face, still panting.

"Yyyes," I stammered.

"You know that Juden are not allowed in public parks, don't you?!" he shouted hysterically at the top of his voice.

"I was only crossing."

"But you are here, and you are not supposed to be here, isn't it so?" He's authoritarian and trying to sound grown up. His shouting attracted the attention of the strollers, and I saw them in the corner of my eyes coming closer and watching us.

"Klaus, don't you remember me?" I tried to sound conciliatory. "We used to play baseball together, just a few weeks ago," I added in a faltering voice.

"Shut your mouth, you filthy Jude. Why would I want to play with a Jude?" He kept on stressing the "Jude", shouting it louder for the benefit of the gapers, especially those in uniform. He uttered it with such loathing as if it alone were infected with the plague. "We have no use for Juden, just as you have no use for us Germans."

"Bbbbut we always got along." I protested meekly, trying to placate him.

"Shut up, you *dreckische* (filthy) Jude!" he raised the whip threateningly. "That's before I knew you Juden were against us and that you really hate us and that you'd like to see our Fuehrer, Adolf Hitler, defamed."

"But I don't hate you. Our family has great respect for Germans, and so do I," I said. "I even respect Hitler for his daring conq…" I caught myself in time, realizing that "conquest" may not be exactly the way Germans regarded Hitler's seizure of Austria, Czechoslovakia and Poland. Their propaganda claimed that their sneak attack on Poland was provoked and, hence, a justifiable defense move.

"You lie! You Juden are all liars!" The gawkers were growing in size and getting closer. "You'll say anything to throw us off-track. You, Juden, are a race of liars. And you do hate us, you liar!" The slash of his whip was so fast that only after a sharp burning on my left cheek I realized that he whipped me. My eyes filled with tears.

"But we don't. It's the truth. I don't hate you, really. I want to stay friends with you."

Another singeing lash of the whip caught me across the neck.

"You hate us! You hate us! *Du hasst uns!*" he shouted in German for the benefit of the onlookers. "You filthy, lying, *drekische* Jude!" he sputtered in Polish and German and whisked his whip again, but this time I caught it and quickly wrapped it around my hand trying to yank it out of his. But the Hitler Youth tightened his grip to keep from being pulled toward me. His faded blue eyes were blazing with hatred. His straight blond locks tousled on his forehead. I returned his glare, no longer certain about my good will toward him or to the Germans in general. My eyes swelled with tears of helpless anger. With a sudden jerk he tugged at the whip, and I let up on my grip, yet alert and ready to dodge the next lash. But he spun around and haughtily walked away. He turned to me once more and shouted really loud: "And don't you ever set foot in this park again, you filthy Jude." While passing the gapers and soldiers, he addressed them in German: "This *drekische* Jude has learned his lesson and won't ever defile our park with his stinking presence."

Watching him disappear, I nodded, muttering to myself: "Yes, yes, you're right, Klaus. I do hate you," and quickly made my way to the exit.

Why did he pick on me? We used to play here together. We never had any fights. Not even disagreements. Why did I suddenly become his arch enemy? Polish Christians weren't barred from public parks. And now Klaus guarded their decorum by keeping them from being defiled by Jews.

That was the last time I saw my beloved park. The scuffle left me with a really bad memory of it. All the fun days there were now tainted with my disgraceful banishment. My ego wouldn't be as bruised if I could only fight that hateful Hitler Youth, just as I once fought some Polish kids who berated me with anti-Semitic slurs a year before the war.

A group of boys, about eleven years of age, like me, in uniforms of a neighboring Skorupki School, started hurling anti-Semitic insults at us from across the street as we were leaving our Katznelson Academy building. I had that sudden sunken feeling that I am not as good as others in the human species; not equal to them – the Christian Poles, who didn't know me personally, yet felt empowered enough to belittle me with bigoted insults. They were goading us to a fight, but my classmates turned a deaf ear and just kept walking home. I, however, in a truly reckless mood, ran out towards them and accepted their challenge. My classmates tried to dissuade me, but I stood firm, deciding to fight one of the Polish boys just to prove they were wrong about Jews being chicken. They accepted my challenge. We went in to a nearby tenement gateway. My classmates quickly vanished. The Poles chose one of their big schoolmates to fight me. We lay our satchels down, and I threw myself at the rugged youth with a fury that I didn't believe I had. He shielded his face from my attack. My fists kept landing on his elbows and other bony protrusions, but I, immune to pain, just kept flailing as if in a trance, my arms and fists loaded with indestructible force; the jaw of an ass in the hands of a Samson, an unexplained force slaying the Philistines. The Christian boys stood by, fascinated, keeping their distance and just rooting for their big pal. I was encouraged when their "Beat the Kike!" faded into mere obscenities. My daring must have impressed them enough to drop their anti-Semitic slurs. Until then, they must have regarded a Jew as a coward and not a fighter.

We fell into a clinch and, as we struggled to topple each other, the cheering abruptly stopped. I peaked from under his armpit and saw the stern face of Principal Dabrowski, towering over us and flanked by my classmates who apparently fetched him. We instantly loosened our stranglehold, withdrew and straightened up. My opponent and his buddies promptly vanished while I was taken to our principal's office and kept there for a long time until one of my parents came for me. I was suspended from school for three days. In the eyes of our school administration, a brawling pupil had to be duly punished, notwithstanding his lofty motives. Mama and Dad were pained at my fracas and suspension because they paid a steep tuition for my education at that private school.

My good intentions to discourage anti-Semitic slander ended shamefully. But I consoled myself with the thought that I dared to put the bigoted boys in their place. With the Hitler Youth, I regrettably couldn't draw such consolation.

Chapter 12:
These Crafty Jews

Will we work again under Jews like in the ghetto or under the Germans in Germany? My first experience of working directly under the Germans, when I was twelve, was frightful.

A few weeks after the German conquest of Lodz, I was walking on some errand for Mama near our pre-war home. A bright yellow armband was on my upper left sleeve, which even Jewish children had to wear. German military trucks were busily confiscating Jewish property all over Lodz, even in the absence of their owners. Soldiers from various military branches would enter a store, a warehouse, or a factory, and promptly remove the whole stock onto their trucks. It seemed as if their main objective of conquering Poland was to plunder the Jews. They reveled in such looting and grabbed Jewish pedestrians to load the "confiscated" goods onto their trucks. Whenever a Jew espied a military truck in front of a Jewish business, he prudently kept far away lest he, too, be forced to join the loaders.

That's why, spotting such a scene in some distance, I quickened my pace in the opposite direction to avoid being grabbed, although the Germans never picked twelve year olds. But, it was too late. A soldier, posted on a street corner to round up Jews, noticed me and gave chase waving and yelling at the top of his voice, the sense of which I couldn't make out because he was almost a block away. But, in those tumultuous days, I wasn't about to be detained from doing an errand for Mama in the neighborhood store and let her worry. I started walking even faster but still didn't dare to run as this might have riled the German and provoke him to shoot at me. Like a mouse into a hole, I darted into the nearest gateway of a huge tenement, gasping, sweating, and hoping that he'd quit chasing me as I could have easily vanished into one of the hundreds of flats. My heart was pounding. My mind was frantically searching for any friends living in that building where I could take cover. I dreaded the thought that he followed me and could discover me hiding behind the gate. The seconds dragged on forever. I already wanted to peek out into the street to check if the coast was clear and make sure that he gave up his hunt for me. Surely, he won't be searching for me in all these flats. The streets were rife with adults, so why should he chase after a boy? He probably grabbed someone else already. I finally caught my breath. I sighed deeply. The danger was surely over.

At once, I froze numb with fear! There he was! Inside the gateway! Right before me, grasping a rifle, flush and panting, but pleased with himself for having caught up with his elusive prey who dared to foil a German superman. I caught a look of surprise on his flared-up face. He probably thought he was pursuing an adult, not a twelve-year-old. My age probably saved me from some serious punishment; he just grabbed me by the coat collar and triumphantly led me to the trucks.

There, together with some fifteen other Jews, all grown-ups, I had to walk up four flights of stairs where German soldiers kept piling stacks of clothing bolts on my outstretched arms. I strained under the weight. I reeled. The stacks were up to my nose, which kept me from seeing the stairs on my way down, but I stepped carefully and didn't drop my load. Those who shed a single bolt got a severe beating from the soldiers posted along the stairs to oversee the operation. I had never carried anything that heavy. Yet, even though the weight taxed my spine to the breaking point, I did it. I showed that despite my age, I was able to carry the loads without once dropping any or falling, although, I did stumble a few times. It was dreadful slaving like this while the soldiers kept amusing themselves by rushing us, delivering occasional blows and taunting us that at last Jews were performing honest labor.

When I came up for my third load, the officer in charge of the confiscation snapped at me: "*Komm mal hier, los!* (Come here, quickly!)". Hopeful that he might discharge me because of my age, I briskly stepped up to him. "*Zieh mal den Mantel aus, los!* (Take off the coat, quickly!)", he commanded pointing at my winter overcoat. And before I even had a chance to react, one of the soldiers jerked it off me and handed it to the officer who turned it over, and burst out laughing, showing the soldiers what amused him so. My fur collar deceived him; he assumed that my whole coat was lined with fur, but it was only a narrow fur-strip buttoned down on top of the cloth collar, just for show to give it a prosperous look.

Had it been fur, the officer would have confiscated it because Jews had to relinquish all furs as well as foreign currency, cars, gold and radios, just to mention a few. His adjutants joined him in a chorus of laughter. "These crafty Jews," he snickered half in contempt and half in approbation, but returned my coat to me, obviously regarding it unworthy of confiscating.

Finally, when the warehouse had been emptied, I was released, came home, and told Mama what happened. She was worried sick over my prolonged absence and dismayed that her only child could be taken from her at any time and any place. I didn't even tell her how heavy the loads were so she wouldn't worry too much.

But now I'm seventeen already and, at least, better prepared for physical exertion if I'll have to do forced labor under direct German supervision again.

Chapter 13:
Cards and Discussions

When the Germans confined us to our homes in the first weeks of their occupation, we resorted to playing cards from the sheer lack of anything else to do. Dad played rummy with our next-door neighbor, Theodor Ryder, an orchestra conductor married to a German Christian who once sang in opera and was still quite attractive. Mr. Ryder was a distinguished middle-age gentleman with a goatee, always well dressed, very composed and never got upset at his bad luck. They played for hours because of a curfew for Jews from 9:00 in the evening until the next morning. Jews also couldn't travel, so Dad was home, as was Mr. Ryder because Jewish musicians couldn't perform. But they played absent-mindedly and often engaged in discussions of our precarious situation.

These talks were always about the German love of militarism since the Crusades and how their passionate nationalism was ignited when Bismarck unified Germany and how it replaced their contributions to Humanism. Dad maintained that the Germans found a good feeling in Fascism, with its parades, solemn rites and spectacles. Their saber-rattling showed the world that they were still a power to reckon with, even though their brilliant contributions in philosophy, literature and music fizzled out in the 19th century. Unable to make any further imprint on the world in these fields, they chose to excel in military conquest so exceptional that it would surpass those of Genghis Khan, Alexander the Great and Napoleon. After all, they were the true sons of the Goths and the Crusaders. Under Hitler, they'd prove that they're still masters. If they can't dominate the world in culture and in peace, they'll do it in war. Hitler's frustration at becoming an artist surely must have had something to do with it. If he couldn't create anything worthwhile in the arts, then he'd destroy better than anyone else.

Dad and Mr. Ryder consented that Hitlerism was an example of a frustrated nation feeding itself with the myth that because of its superior achievements in technology or art, it is so gifted that it towers over all other nations solely by its inherent racial stock. Hitler feeds the Germans an exalted concept of themselves that they are a legend in their own minds. Their mere racial superiority gives them the right to expand eastward to subjugate inferior Slavs or push westward to control the degenerate French. "If you exalt yourself but think of others as inferior, soon you'll find them unfit to be your neighbors or even dwell anywhere on Earth except six feet under it," Dad said forebodingly.

Later, in the ghetto, Mr. Ryder became the orchestra conductor when our cultural life somewhat resurfaced. His music kept up our spirits. Good musical revues were staged in the only theater. Mama, who always loved the stage and the movies, took me to one of the performances, which I enjoyed in spite of my hungry and tugging stomach.

Mr. and Mrs. Ryder were much in love despite their middle-age. She would sometimes come over to fetch him from his card playing, then stay for tea and a chat. She was a German-Christian, yet chose to follow him into the ghetto and share the fate of all Jews even though the Nazis had given her the option to divorce him and leave him to his lot.

Banished from parks and schools and not forced to work yet while only thirteen years of age, we, the budding teenagers, were reduced into idleness in the beginning of the ghetto. A boy could either read books or play cards to find a diversion. Both helped to escape reality. A winning streak in a card game provided a much needed relief from our losses in real life, proving that ill fortune was temporary; if one stayed in the game, he could yet persevere. The trick was to endure. Endure hunger until the next meal, often days away, endure exile until quotas stop, endure the shootings, the hangings, the deaths of loved ones.

We played obsessively, disregarding everything around us. At least the games that involved certain strategies offered us some degree of control. With the world irrational and descending into chaos, card games remained the only constant, proving that fortunes fluctuate; we expected this with a passion whenever we were down on our luck. We even tried to evoke good fortune by conjuring Lady Luck, our Lucky Star or even God Himself. We also resorted to a kind of mysticism by seeking hidden meanings in the numerical value of cards or numbers and letters of the alphabets, to discover some inherent order of events in this world. Perhaps we didn't really search for a magic way to win at cards as to prove to ourselves that there was some order and meaning in life, and that in this seemingly haphazard and mystical universe, there was a guiding light, if only numerical, which could attest to the existence of The One who devised it all. Didn't the ancients seek meaning in configurations of stars and drawing them into figures of Gods, thereby seeking messages from the sky as if it were a conclave of their deities?

Later, in the ghetto, a certain Mr. Sonnenberg opened a private library across the street at 43 Zgierska Street, and I was able to immerse myself in reading again. However, card playing and reading both had to stop. Our situation became so desperate that even I, at thirteen, had to find a job to be eligible for food rations that were allotted to workers only.

Chapter 14:
Ousted from Home

Just a few weeks into the Nazi rule, we were evicted from our pre-war home. A German military officer entered our apartment with a Volksdeutsche couple. The woman held a baby in her arms. They spoke German to us, yet as ethnic Germans, they surely could speak Polish. But my parents could speak German, too. They ordered us out of our home immediately, confining us into our narrow kitchen for two days until we found some other quarters. The kitchen had a separate entrance from the hall. They gave us half an hour to gather our bedding, clothing and other bare necessities, but no furniture.

Oh, no! Not my treasured desk! My huge desk made of fine, heavy wood with roll-up panels that covered six rows of drawers on each side; it was a gift from Grandpa on my eleventh birthday a year ago so that I could do my homework at it undisturbed instead of doing it at the dining room table, a possession that was all mine, a corner in the apartment virtually my own, that, in a way, established my independence. Sometimes Dad would sit at it, too, to write a business letter in his elaborate calligraphic flourishes. But, otherwise, it was all mine, my prized possession, this precious piece of furniture.

The civilian, short and skinny, glared at us oozing hatred, as if we had personally done him some terrible wrong. He pointed at other furniture pieces, starting with my parents' king-size bed, and the huge wardrobe, and barked out peremptorily: "*Dass gehoert uns!* (This belongs to us!)". His scowl seemed to say: You filthy Jews stole it all from decent Christian folk like us. Now we're repossessing it! His plump wife, holding the infant, kept pointing her head and chin to paintings and at whatever else that struck her fancy, chiming in with a cackle: "*Und das auch! Und das! Und das auch! Alles dieses gehoert uns!* (And this too! And this! And this too! All of these belong to us!)".

The tall hefty officer warned my parents not to touch anything that has been pointed out or they'd suffer the consequences, upon which Dad began to plead with him over something in a small chest, maybe Mama's jewelry. But the officer drew his gun and menacingly shook it at Dad, telling him not to protest. Mama became mortified at the sight of the drawn gun, and pleaded with Dad not to object.

When Dad took out from the wardrobe a velvet pouch with his phylacteries and the tallit, the runty Volksdeutsch pounced on him with such vehemence as if he caught Dad stealing from him. He, his wife and the officer ordered Dad to empty the contents of the pouch and watched intently as he did so, obviously expecting to discover a treasure in jewels, cash, or valuables of some sort. A look of disappointment and incredulity passed over their faces when Dad pulled out his phylacteries. They picked up and examined the two leather boxes, lifting and turning the little cubicles, checking them out from all sides and weighing them in their hands, and finally trying to rip them open. Dad winced and made a sudden move toward the short and puny German who darted for protection toward the tall officer, complaining: "*Der Judenschwein wird ungeduldig* (The Jewish swine is becoming impatient)." Dad explained that it was only a praying attachment and of no possible use for the German couple.

"Oh, yeah? We'll see about that," said the cocky little German, emboldened by the officer's gun and his menacing presence, and ripped the tiny box apart. Out fell a tiny scroll with a Hebrew prayer on it. He picked it up for a closer scrutiny, but couldn't make it out, so he crumpled it and tossed it on the floor, muttering something about "*verdammte Juden* (accursed Jews.)", surely disappointed that this object, so precious to Dad, was of no use to him.

Dad picked up the scroll, shaking his head at such sacrilege. I waited for God to smite the German for his outrageous act. But nothing happened. Dejected, I started emptying my desk and collecting my books and toys. The officer focused his attention on me and a death-mask I had on my desk: a scary looking yellow skull with grinning teeth. He ordered me to hand it over, checked it out on the inside and placed it on my face. My big, fear-stricken eyes, peeking out from the two hollow cavities, must have seemed quite amusing to him for he let out a guffaw. Then he took it off my face and still laughing, handed it back to me. Just like Dad's phylacteries, this was of no use to him.

We had to surrender the key from the inside kitchen door and the officer put an official tape across it, strictly forbidding us to damage it. Stunned, we sat in the narrow kitchen now crammed with bedding, clothing, books and my toys. Only six months earlier, before the war, we moved into this second floor apartment because it was just a short walk from Grandpa's factory, it faced the street, and it was in a nice, quiet neighborhood. Unlike the previous tenement where there were many Jewish residents, this one seemed to be occupied mostly by Christians. Perhaps that's why we were evicted so soon after the German take over – Jews weren't welcome among Christians anymore, especially Jews residing in choice locations. Our neighbors across the hall, the Weiss family, were not evicted probably because their small flat faced the yard. Next to them lived a childless middle-aged couple – the noted orchestra conductor Theodor Ryder, who was Jewish but was not evicted probably because his wife was a German Aryan and a former diva.

The sudden surrender of family heirlooms and jewelry to the predatory Volksdeutsche couple had dire consequences a year later. From all my parents' and Grandpa's furniture and things, Dad managed to salvage only our down comforters and pillows, a real blessing, because they kept us warm in an unheated room the next five ghetto winters.

Now, unfortunately, we're without them. Only knapsacks are allowed on this journey. We'll miss the bedding. Who knows in what bed we'll be sleeping tonight?

After our eviction into the kitchen, we slept there on the floor. Afraid that the Germans might grab our comforters, too, Dad hired a droshky that came at night and parked on the street below our kitchen window. Then he tossed out to the coachman each piece of bedding one by one. It was a dreadful night. Dad didn't want to leave the hateful couple anything else of value, so he even tried to burn up our whole supply of coals and kept piling them into the kitchen stove that night and the next until we were ordered to vacate the kitchen as well. The three of us were sweltering but Dad wouldn't rest and just kept the oven going. He lost two nights of sleep but in his small way he deprived the hoggish Volksdeutsche of most of our coal supply.

How will Mama and I sleep in the cold without those life-savings blankets? Oh, well, it's the end of August, so we won't miss them till winter, and by then maybe we'll finally be liberated from these heartless Hitlerites.

Chapter 15:
A Small Miracle

...staccato, staccato, staccato...

...the covers, the covers, the covers...

Our most prized possession from pre-war prosperity, life savers from freezing, now they, too, are gone. How will we survive another harsh winter without them? What miracle will save us now? It's a miracle that Mama and I are still together, surviving. It'll be an even bigger miracle if Mama and I outlast this Hitlerite scourge, not just a small one like the one our family shared about Great-Grandfather's evading a German's abuse.

One of the German soldiers' main recreations was cutting off the beards and side-locks of orthodox Jews. Sometimes, they would also demand that such a Jew remove his skullcap and shine their boots with it. One would think that a bearded Jew in traditional dark clothing was a personal affront to them. They zealously singled out such Jews for special humiliation. Why was Jewish devotion to God provoking them to such a rage? Were they testing our God to prove His existence by coming to our rescue as in Biblical times? And they always chose our major holidays to torment us as if to prove that we had been abandoned by our God as His so-called Chosen People.

One of these malevolent soldiers with a pair of scissors in hand, seeking fun with bearded Jews, ran into my great-grandfather. Shlomo Mayer Bodzechowski vel Eichorn was as imposing in person as in his lengthy name. A tall, stately and vigorous man in his mid-eighties, he walked erect and sprightly, even though he had a walking stick, which he probably used as a symbol of his advanced age rather than for physical support. Perhaps he even used it to defend himself when accosted by Polish hooligans, who, before the war, also liked to pick on elderly Jews in traditional garb and pull their beards, sidelocks, or simply give them a whack and keep walking. He had clear blue eyes and a patriarchal, sprawling white beard, which, together with his cane, made him look like Moses with his divining rod. I used to see him at Grandma's where he sometimes visited, although I don't recall him ever talking to me. He was always in a rush and probably had no time to waste on me. He was a remarried widower known for his piety, virtue and Talmudic study. He had begotten eight daughters including Grandma and only one son, Joel, whom he had driven so hard to Bible study that Joel, at thirteen, ran away from home first to England and then to the USA.

And there he was striding with his cane on the streets of Lodz in 1940, on a collision course with the Teutonic Warrior/Aryan *Uebermensch* (Superman). The German stopped him, grabbed his full white beard, raising the scissors for cutting when the unexpected took place, which our family regarded as a small miracle. Great-Grandfather raised his eyebrows, and, widely opening his clear blue eyes, looked the German square in the face, then lifted his hand and without a single word shook his finger in a forbidding gesture. The German must have been astounded by such a brazen reaction from the old Jew. But apparently, he was taken aback, for, lo and behold, he hesitated, lowered his hand with the scissors and, also without a word, motioned Great-Grandfather to go on his way with his beard still intact. In his "struggle" (*Mein Kampf*) against Jews, Hitler lost this little round against an old Jew who scored a victory by getting to keep his beard and perhaps some pieces of flesh that usually went with it by the scissors of eager and sadistic soldiers.

Chapter 16:
Trapped

...the ghetto, the ghetto, the ghetto...

But those first months of German occupation of Lodz were not the worst yet. The Hitlerites, ever more cruel, forced us into an overcrowded slum, starved us to death, executed us by hangings, shot at us for walking near the barbed-wire fence, and took away little children from their parents.

In February of 1940 they evicted two-hundred thousand of us from our homes in city proper and forced us into an area without running water or sewage. It was an epic migration. Jews, forbidden to hire a cab or a horse-pulled lorry, carried things on their backs or dragged them through the snow on makeshift carts, rushing frantically to beat the deadline and move into the ghetto before the Germans would burst into their homes and shoot people outright. We were trapped, caged, distraught and at the mercy of brutal killers.

They crowded us three families per room or about nine people. My parents and I shared our two rooms at 38 Zgierska Street with the four Lawits (Mama's third younger sister Andzia, her husband Ignatz, and their two young daughters) and two Maliniaks (Great Aunt Rozia and her husband Aaron). Others had to share their rooms with total strangers. Aaron's incessant cough and cigar smoking even at night drove the four Lawits into the narrow kitchen where they remained for the next four years. Aaron soon vanished and Rozia moved in with her sister Dvoira, whose husband Baruch Bodzechowski occupied a whole flat with his family because he held an important position as a bakery manager.

I once stood in line for bread at his bakery where I got clubbed by a Jewish policeman who was keeping order. Uncle Baruch didn't know that I was in that heaving line to spare me the clubbing or my hunger. And they ran out of bread before I even got inside. Aunt Rozia, meanwhile, without her resourceful husband Aaron, survived the first years of starvation with food packages from her two boys in the USSR until June of 1941, when Hitler turned on his allies and all mail into the ghetto stopped.

The first three years of steady German victories didn't assuage their blood-thirst. It raged on in our ghetto with random shootings, hangings, forcible starvation and deportations. As for the body count, the ghetto, our miserable cage, was practically a war zone itself. They took it out on us, who were like animals in our miserable trap. To keep Poles away, posters at the barbed wires, warned that our territory was contaminated with typhus, while in truth, most of us were dying of starvation. We were sealed off hermetically. Even radios were banned and listening to one was punishable by death. Yet, with all those who died, our overcrowding was unrelieved because of constant transports of Jews from Germany, Austria and Czechoslovakia. In November of '41, about five thousand gypsies were also sent in and kept separate from us; we could hear their agonizing cries when we walked near the wires of their ghetto within a ghetto; but after some months, all of them suddenly disappeared.

The ghetto was an anachronism from the Middle Ages. And the yellow badges, too. But so was war. That's what everybody thought after World War I until 1939 when Poland was again robbed of its independence. To me and my school friends, that earlier war with its horror tales was just history. Even though our parents lived through it some twenty years ago, to us it seemed as distant as the Napoleonic wars. We read about it as a lesson that the civilized world would not ever allow to be repeated. When we saw a movie about it, we weren't scared any more than when seeing a horror film with monsters.

Chapter 17:
Resettlements and Deportations

...the ghetto, the ghetto, the ghetto...

"**A**re you all right, Mietek?" Mama asks. I'm angry with myself for letting out a groan, but a sharp pain pierces the arch of my right foot lodged under someone.

"Yeah, I'm okay." I answer gruffly, so that no one would think of me as a mama's boy. Everybody around is depressed and mangled, and she has to treat me like a little boy! She has enough to worry about such as her sisters and their young children who left on earlier transports.

The August night is hot and sticky. The stench of human waste from the vat permeates the whole car. But at least the train keeps moving so we'll soon arrive and be out of this misery. Roll faster away from that ghastly ghetto...the ghetto...the ghetto...

Mama and I we were able to evade deportations as much as we could. But avoiding this final one meant instant death if we got caught. A similar threat faced us also four years ago in 1940 if we refused to abandon our pre-war homes and move into the ghetto together with thousands of other Jews who were herded in from other Western countries. They told us stories, much like our own, of loss and humiliation, of being jeered in their native towns where they had lived for centuries, of confiscated businesses, and eviction from the comfort and safety of their homes. Some of their Christian neighbors readily denounced them in order to profit from their abandoned properties. They were berated for being different – aliens of a despised race, religion, customs; yet they behaved and dressed exactly like everyone else. They told us of Nazi propaganda films that portrayed Jews as hordes of rats carrying infectious diseases and depicted Jewish types of men with homely, gaunt faces, long, narrow hooked noses and narrow eyes, and grim or cunning expressions. Uncle Sym noted that if one looks for caricatures of people, it would be easy enough to find a German type with bulky snub noses, slit eyes, and round faces set on thick necks, the total effect being that of a pig's snout.

But while we, in the Lodz Ghetto, have already grown accustomed to our misery, these "Westerners" have not. Our squalor overwhelmed them and they became even more wretched than we were. Many committed suicide. We commiserated with them as they quickly disintegrated. And yet, they fared better than the Eastern Jews who, according to rumors, were routed up near the Russian-German frontier, stripped naked, shot and thrown into pits. But we thought that maybe the Germans themselves spread these rumors just to keep us complacent about our miserable lot.

Once, in 1943, Mama and I had been summoned for a deportation, but we quickly hid out for some ten days with hardly any food while sleeping in some strange, one-room little cottage in the remote and desolate area of Marysin until the quota was filled and the transport left. We couldn't stay with our relatives because, if the police found us there, they, too, would be deported as punishment for giving us shelter. It was a nightmarish experience, running and hiding like tracked animals and yet staying with Mama all this time eased my terror. That time, at least, we weathered the storm and could return to our room on Zgierska Street to continue living under the same roof with Aunt Andzia, and not too far away from Aunt Asta with her family, and Aunt Hela with Uncle Sym.

But that was two years ago. Deportations weren't final then like this one with no hope of waiting it out anymore. I just hope that I remain together with Mama.

Chapter 18:
The Bridge

Zgierska Street was the ghetto's main thoroughfare for Aryan traffic. It was fenced-off by barbed wire on both sidewalks to keep Jews from crossing. A three-story high wooden bridge was constructed so that Jews could cross from one side of the ghetto to the other. Climbing that bridge became another hurdle in the ever worsening ghetto existence. German sentries, posted every hundred meters alongside the barbed wire fence, made sure that no Jew got out. Occasionally, these sentries shot and killed Jewish pedestrians who might have gotten too close to the wires or who lingered on the bridge.

Poles and Germans in the passing streetcars viewed us with a curiosity reserved for zoo animals. Some boys pointed at us and jeered, laughing at times, though there was nothing funny about us except our emaciation. Our clothes were the same as worn by the people on the outside except for the yellow stars sewn on our outside garments. The fleeting presence of the well-fed people on the streetcars reminded us that there still was a normal world out there with motorized traffic and people going about their usual business. Then we felt even more isolated and haggard in our ghetto cage.

Some despondent Jews, probably wanting to alert the world of our miserable plight, jumped off the bridge under the oncoming trolleys. This accursed structure caused many of us to faint or die from exhaustion as well.

The relentless hunger in 1941 was intensified by a cold winter in our unheated room. The Germans rationed briquettes in very small allotments as if trying to punish us by freezing us to death in addition to starvation. And many people did die of exposure. I, and hundreds of others, scavenged wood from old fences and dilapidated buildings, but soon the Germans outlawed this, too, just to make life more unbearable for us. By then, practically all empty wooden structures in the ghetto had already been dismantled anyway, and people began to burn up good furniture just to keep from freezing to death.

Once I, too, nearly succumbed to exhaustion while carrying a sack of briquettes over that damned bridge. The ration for the whole winter had to be redeemed one time only, and I carried it on my back from several streets away. But the worst part was hauling the load across that troublesome bridge. Weakened from hunger, I always struggled to climb it, even without the heavy sack on my back. But with the coals, it was an exhausting feat that threatened to collapse me. Just tossing that full sack over my shoulders made me stagger. I had to rest often and scale those steep and narrow steps slowly as blood surged to my head from the strain, my hand gripped the railing, my legs went limp, and my heart pounded wildly. To inch forward, I had to use not only my legs, but exert my whole body. It was a monumental effort to carry that load without rest, but one had to be ever wary of the trigger-happy sentry below. Oh, how I wished to sit down for just a minute on those steep stairs to catch my breath. From a youth, bursting with boundless energy, I, at fourteen, changed into a feeble oldster in just a few months.

Each year, when crossing that accursed bridge with my sack of briquettes, I thought it would be my last act on earth. I kept thinking of tiny ants hauling their oversize loads to their mound and telling myself that I must persevere, that I mustn't collapse nor stop, that if tiny ants can haul big weights then so can I. Images of my Hebrew ancestors heaving large stones up the Egyptian pyramids kept flickering through my mind. Even in this much-mourned time in Jewish history, they weren't being starved to death.

Chapter 19:
Dad Starves

Before the war, Szymon Weintraub was a traveling salesman for Lando Textiles in Warsaw and was related to its owners. Tall and stout, with a shaven head, an open face and a narrow, patrician nose, Dad was used to eating well and suffered the sudden hunger more than the rest of us. To get food rations, Dad had to find a job just like everyone else, and got one as a loader in a vegetable freight yard, shoveling turnips, carrots, beets, rutabagas and whatever else was to be distributed to food cooperatives. He'd come home exhausted and ravenous, pleading with Mama for some food. But there wasn't any.

His bulk was soon gone, and he became emaciated. Like a helpless child, in a thin, plaintive voice, he begged for food as if Mama kept it from him. It was degrading for this big man to speak in that tone of voice. I felt embarrassed for him as I recalled how strong and melodious his voice once was. Mama kept adding water to already thin soups, which he'd gobble up in an instant. Often she had nothing with which to feed him but a pot of weak ersatz coffee to fill his empty stomach. But this wasn't nourishing, and he began eating up most of our total weekly allotment of bread. Then Mama started dividing the two kilo loaf and put his third share separately. But he'd wolf it down in one sitting and then nibble at our portions for the rest of the week. It didn't help Mama to hide our bread in pillow cases or towels, among linens or behind books on my bookshelves. He'd find it everywhere. It didn't even help when Mama called him a "shameless thief" and "child murderer, depriving your own growing boy of his nourishment." Oblivious to her, with a blank stare in his sunken eyes, he'd go on gobbling up our shares on the sly.

"You should sacrifice yourself for your child instead of stealing from him," she'd reproach him utterly exasperated. She was giving up most of her portions to feed me. But Dad didn't pay her any heed. "The mice ate it," he'd reply, and impatiently wave his hand as if chasing away a pesky fly. Mice indeed sometimes got at the hidden bread, gnawing it up from the inside, while here it was obvious that the portions got smaller by human hands. I even bought a mousetrap that caught mice live with a drop of the trap door of the cage. But a piece of sausage or a crumb of bread was too precious a morsel to waste, even at the price of catching a pilfering mouse.

The hunger was relentless and exhausting. My stomach, churning in pain, kept feeding on its own tissue. We'd go on for two or three days with nothing to put in our mouths. Sleeping – if I could manage to fall asleep for even a few minutes – was a restless dream, a delirious vision of food, mainly of bread, of chewing and swallowing and swallowing wholesome, filling gulps that would appease that gnawing, howling hollow inside of me.

At first, I, too, went to work in a vegetable yard though not to tend lorries like Dad, but as a gofer. Mama pulled me out of school, and got me this job through some favor; any work near food improved survival. Indeed, at times I'd eat a carrot on the sly, but it was risky; anything in the yard was public property; if the Germans found out, it could be punishable by death. I soon lost that good job anyway. The yard's steward, Mr. Handler, a handsome married man, was charged with stealing public property. I, too, was involved for carrying the stolen goods for him. He'd send me on errands to his beautiful lover who lived several streets away. I'd bring her pots full of hot soup, pieces of wood for heating, or whatever other items he filled the basket with. But soon the jig was up. Someone reported the theft; I was fired and investigated about the contents of the baskets. But seeing a naive messenger boy, they found me innocent. Losing this job and an occasional carrot was disastrous as I again became dependent on the meager food rations.

Dad was wasting away rapidly. He had no pride left. Once a relaxed and jovial man, he became nervous, erratic and concerned only with food; mostly talking about it or reminiscing how it once tasted. This increased the flow of saliva to his empty stomach, filling it for just a moment and easing the hunger. Soon we all did it to stave off the pangs that returned with a vengeance as soon as the increased saliva flow subsided. Dad's usual relaxed behavior became fidgety, and his eyes darted feverishly from one object to another as if in a frantic search for food. The ersatz coffee without any sugar or milk gave him only a short relief, just like saliva, bloating him instead. His feet and legs swelled up. This slowed down his walking, which got him fired from his job in the yard. Now he was also deprived of a furtive bite on a carrot or turnip in the watery soup dished out for lunch to all ghetto workers at their work places. He had to be laid up.

Mother had to find some work to save the three of us from starving to death. She got a job, peeling potatoes in a soup kitchen. This helped a little because she was allowed to bring home some rotten potato peels, which after much washing, soaking, scrubbing, and rinsing, she'd turn into some edible dish that kept us from starving. But Dad's condition got worse. Mama got a second job, at night, in a matzah bakery but couldn't bring anything to eat. Dad was fading away. The swelling in his legs moved up to his torso.

I, too, stayed in my bed after work just to preserve energy and to keep warm in that unheated room during the fierce winter of 1941. Luckily we salvaged our goose-down comforters, and I kept my head under them so that my breath would warm me up faster. But even they couldn't protect us from the elements outside because March and April brought down the rains, and our ceiling started leaking right onto our beds and us.

It was painful to watch Dad's deterioration. One night, when his usual whimpering stopped, I was relieved that he finally went to sleep. But when Mama returned from her bakery job at dawn, she found him unconscious. Frantically she ran down to fetch Dr. Cukier, a neighbor. He came up at once and gave Dad a shot of something that caused his whole body to quiver in convulsions. His laborious breath changed to a death rattle, and his eyes rolled up. The shot failed to bring him back. The doctor left. Helpless, we watched Dad's final agony. When the doctor returned soon, it was over, and he wrote out a death certificate. The cause: malnutrition. The swelling had reached Dad's heart and disabled it.

What happened next shocked me because it was so unexpected. As soon as the doctor left, Mama ran up to the window facing the vast courtyard, flung it open, and let out a piercing, painful wail. Was this some kind of ancient ritual? How could this modern lady make such a public scene? I thought that a death of a close relative should be suffered quietly, privately and undemonstratively. But such an overt display of grief startled me. "Woe is me! Woe is me! My husband Szymon is dead!" she yelled in a howl as penetrating as the freezing drizzle gusting into our room. Surely everyone in the tenement must have heard her. But dying before one's time was not unusual in our sprawling complex at 38 Zgierska Street where thousands of people crammed in hundreds of rooms had been starving to death for a year. I wanted to drag her away from that open window, but I was too self-conscious. There must have been hundreds staring at Mama from windows or from the yard near the water pump where people always lined up to fill their pails. Was anyone really moved by her wail when so many of them had recently lost their loved ones, or did they think: "So the Angel of Death found his way to your house, too? Now you know how we feel." No one showed up to offer a hug, a handshake or even sympathy.

Mama left me with Dad's corpse in the room and probably went to arrange for his burial. Numbed, I stood before my bookshelves. How could such a healthy and stout man die so quickly without really being sick? He used to razz me whenever I had the flu or something that he had never been sick in his life, not even with a cold or a cough. I didn't cry, sure that real sadness would come later after the initial shock. Now I was more concerned with growing up fatherless so soon after turning fourteen. I tried to focus on the books and detach myself from this event and steer my mind away from the bleak future and a heartsick mother. The war separated her from a supportive and loving father and two warmhearted brothers, and now she was a widow, too. How will she cope without all her relatives' help, money or anything valuable to trade for food?

Dad was always relaxed and couldn't deal with that aggressiveness that was so necessary for survival in the ghetto. He was used to a gentility of normal life, discussing politics or opera over a glass of tea with business associates or friends. At home, he often sang arias and cantorials in his melodious voice. He seemed content with his life, but Mama often chided him for his small earnings that couldn't pay for my private school, and that she, unlike her well-married sisters, had to eke out a living and work. Leafing absentmindedly through my books, I kept hoping that it was all unreal and that Dad would recover and return to his usual self. But nothing happened, and gloom filled the room.

Mama returned with two men who took Dad's swollen corpse out of bed and put it on the dining room table, washed it, then wrapped it with a sheet or shroud. I tried not to watch their gruesome work. Soon they left with Mama who probably went to arrange for a funeral. Dad's wrapped body was on the table. I stared at my books. Suddenly, I was startled by a noise from the corpse. A sigh? A moan? I shuddered. I looked at the shroud, hoping to see it twitch or show a sign of life. Was he coming to? Maybe Dr. Cukier erred? Maybe Dad was recovering? But the shroud remained still. I waited in suspense hoping for another sign of life. None came. I turned to the bookshelves again. The world of fiction was more stable and less chaotic than reality.

Not a soul appeared at Dad's bleak burial. It was just Mama and me, my first burial experience. At the charnel house in the cemetery death had a peculiar stench, probably decomposing flesh. There was a bone-chilling drizzle. The diggers, overworked, exhausted, and unable to keep up with the mass starvation victims, unceremoniously slid Dad's shrouded body from between two man-size boards right into his clayish, wet grave. The gaping hole in that clammy soil engulfed Dad forever, releasing him finally from daily concerns and from responsibility to provide for a wife and worry about his son's future. I was distressed to lose a father, especially to starvation – a pauper's death.

Mama and I felt utterly desolate and chilled in that cold, early April drizzle. How lonely was his return to nothingness. And yet, there must have been hundreds of people who knew Dad, business acquaintances, relatives in Warsaw or Noworadomsk where he was born fifty years ago and who probably attended his circumcision. Where were those who celebrated at his wedding? His bar mitzvah? Who rejoiced at his fatherhood? There he was being buried forever without any of them paying him their last respects. Just another cadaver destined to rot as it merged with the wet, slimy clods of earth, practically anonymous, as if it never existed, the root from which I sprouted. Will his spirit reunite with his parents and grandparents? Will my spirit reunite with his when I die? The burial mystery had been bared to me: a shroud, two planks, the clayey, repellent dirt now lumpier in the rain, and no coffin! I wasn't even sure if it was a Jewish custom or if wood was not available in the ghetto anymore.

What was Hitler's great victory by killing Dad through starvation? He was punishing Jews for being satanic, for scheming, for being parasitic and insect-like, contemptible and yet powerful, for being communists and yet money-grubbers. But Dad did not fit into any of these. Ever cheerful and gentle, he never complained or even grumbled. Powerful?! In his final days on earth, he, in a child's plaintive voice, begged his helpless wife for a morsel of food. Dad died destitute. He left a silver pocket watch on a chain with black Roman numerals on its white face that he always carried in his waistcoat pocket. It probably stopped when Dad died and couldn't be fixed even after I brought it to a watchmaker for repairs. I could only press a button to flip it open and stare at the silver lid with flowers engraved on it and at the dial that stood hopelessly still.

Chapter 20:
The Ghetto Grind

They cordoned us off with barbed wire, posted sentries, and sign-posts:

Wohngebiet der Juden	[Territory of the Jews
Eintrit strengstens verboten	Entry strongly prohibited
TYPHUS	TYPHUS]

From a healthy, vibrant and thriving community, we became a lepers' colony to be avoided like the plague. Some Polish volunteers were appointed as extra sentries around our ghetto and wore navy blue uniforms to distinguish them from the green-uniformed Germans. The Hitlerites always found willing confederates to "put Jews in their place."

"Whoever violates the law will be crushed like lice.
Don't make trouble, but return to your work.
It is warm inside the shops. There is soup.
If you refuse, you'll end up like this garbage."

With these words, Rumkowski pointed to seven men about to be hanged by the SS. It was the first public execution; the whole ghetto had to witness it on the Bazarna Square in February of 1942. Exposing our community to such a cruel sight was barbarism. Wrought in my memory are the woeful eyes of a fifteen-year-old boy standing on the scaffold among the condemned with his wrists tied behind him as the henchmen were putting a noose over his head with his cap still on it. He was a shy and quiet boy, one whom I knew from our soccer games and whom the better players seldom selected for their teams because he lacked aggressiveness. It was hard to believe that this meek and withdrawn boy was capable of any lawbreaking. And he looked at us all with his doleful eyes as if asking, "Why? Why is this happening to me? This can't be for real! And if it is – save me, please. Do something! I don't belong with this group here." At fourteen, I never before saw a person die and tried to shut my eyes. But the Germans threatened us over their loudspeakers to keep our eyes open so that we could learn not to trifle with their ordinances. The assembled crowd gasped as the noose snapped. I avoided looking at his face and just saw his feet twitching for a few endless minutes. I wondered if his parents, too, were forced to be present there with the rest of us to watch his final agony. His budding life was wasted – a warning to us all!

With similar speeches, Rumkowski kept us in check as we were becoming immune to all the those dying us, ever grateful that it wasn't us; that we cheated death if only for another day. How could we grieve and mourn if we could be the next day's victims?

And yet the selections, with their constant pruning of "undesirables" from the ghetto, reassured us that the Hitlerites valued our labor. Rumek kept reiterating that compliance and obedience was all that was left to us, and any protest would result in a blood bath. And we obeyed our Nazi lords and masters, hoping that if we did our work in the shops, they'd let us be – perhaps long enough to endure the Hitler scourge.

In our ghetto, at least, we weren't subjected to random abuse by shears-wielding, sadistic soldiers, nor to sudden seizures for compulsory and abusive labor, nor the degrading doffing of our hats and stepping off the sidewalk before German military personnel. In the ghetto, we were allowed to exist only by our total subservience in the service of the German war effort, with nothing to interfere with performing this duty. That's why it was *verboten* to have babies or small children who'd hamper their parents' labor. Even when slaving for the Egyptian pharaohs – the most gruesome time of our ancient history – Jews were not prevented from having children.

And yet, there were some sadistic soldiers guarding the ghetto who randomly killed Jews walking near the barbed wires. An image of such a killing remained etched in my memory. A young woman was shot at by a sadistic sentry who made her dance before he killed her, though some witnesses claimed that when he aimed his gun at her for no reason at all, she, bewildered, dropped her bundle, tore at her hair, then, flapping her arms and legs, started frenziedly dancing.

And so we tried to keep away from the wires and those lethal sentries as far as we could. Quietly, obediently and forever hungry, we worked in our cold or sweltering shops, then returned to our equally cold or sweltering hovels, and went to our beds to be bitten by millions of bloodsucking bedbugs who probably found our thinned-out blood insufficiently nourishing because they never stopped their nightly assaults, biting, stinging, and sucking. It didn't help scalding the walls with water. Maybe they dropped from the ceiling. Lice, mice and bedbugs were the only critters left in the ghetto. Food was the focus of all our fantasies. Why were the Nazis treating their "productive workers" as if they wanted us *all* to die of starvation?

Even unskilled workers did their share of arduous toil. The most odious of these tasks was the hauling of wagons with excrement. These crews consisted mostly of young boys with an older man, probably their father or uncle, one pulling, the others pushing the fetid tanks through the ghetto streets. They collected their reeking cargo from cesspools of communal toilets in the tenements, then emptied them somewhere on the outskirts of the ghetto. Theirs was a revolting procession. We looked with pity at their grim faces bent low over the soiled metal tanks and at their spindly, bespattered arms, and we held our noses trying not to breathe until they disappeared from view with their loathsome ladings. We shunned them, wishing that they'd get their stinking, slow-moving freight faster out of sight. They were the true lepers in our colony of lepers. And yet, we envied them for their extra ration of soup, rationalizing that their misery was mollified as none of them was starving to death. Did they, too, need connections to land those stinking jobs? While all boys, in order to somehow survive in the ghetto, tried to learn some kind of trade and become skilled at it, those wretches kept stagnating in their repulsive task. How will they fare now, in Germany, without some technical skill? Surely in Germany, cities have sewers, and there's no need for excrement haulers.

Chapter 21:
Ah, the Bread

Again, that nagging hunger. The Hitlerites didn't keep their promise to give us a loaf of bread and marmalade at the station. Many of us showed up for this final deportation voluntarily, without even being dragged out from nooks and crannies, just in hope to still our hunger with their lure. Now we're being shipped off while still starving. Maybe they'll feed us on arrival wherever we're going and ease these pangs. Maybe we will now live among Germans and eat like they do, not having to wait a whole week for that elusive bread, then cut it up into sections to be eaten for the next seven days.

Ah, what a solemn occasion it was when I would finally bring that precious loaf and would sit down at the table with it, cut into its hard crust, slice a piece out of it, and chew heartily before devouring it. But my hunger wouldn't let up. And that piece was to be my whole day's ration. Yet, I ate it all in only one sitting! Maybe I ate it too fast. If I had chewed it more, it would have lasted longer, I reasoned. I'd cut off another slice and savor it for a long time, chewing it until it was liquefied, before letting it drop into my empty stomach. But it still wasn't enough. And the guilt would nag me for depriving myself of tomorrow's ration. Nevertheless, I jammed the knife into it and extracted another slice; although, this time I'd carve out only a small edge of the loaf just to leave it with a more symmetrical shape, I would tell myself. But after eating that morsel, too, I'd carve off yet another edge for the same reason. It was impossible to tear myself away from that tempting loaf. It sat there before me with a power of its own, putting me under its hypnotic spell. Bread was our only regular nourishment because potatoes were rationed much less frequently and horse meat even less. My gaping guts always clamored for more, the digestive juices surged in anticipation of a rare feeding frenzy. But the morsels only increased my appetite. And the luscious loaf would be right before me just sitting there, still in its bulk, and waiting to be chomped and crunched and swallowed and swallowed and swallowed. The loaf fixated itself onto me and wouldn't rest until it found its way into my belly and settle safely inside, before, God forbid, something happened to it! Again I would pick up the knife and pare off another slender piece. Again I would chew ever so slowly, working up enough juices to increase the mass, again the lethal knife pruned a slice, then slow, sensuous chewing, and then another slice. Don't swallow, I would remind myself, prolonging that blissful fullness in the mouth, though my innards screamed for that life-bearing fill to be passed down faster so that my body could start processing it. But I just chewed, working up the saliva to increase each bite to more fullness and deceive that greedy Moloch. I would let it get full on small morsels and lots of pap! As if in a trance, I would carve and chew, carve and chew, hating myself with every cruel cut, and with every knife-plunge into it, it was as if I were killing it, as if it had an existence all of its own. As the loaf was slowly diminishing, I visualized another week of my slow starvation, but hoped that an unexpected ration of potatoes or vegetables would be issued as a windfall to spare me another seven-day fast. The guilt continually gnawed me: How was I going to last a whole week without any food? When I would finally manage to tear myself away from that captivating loaf, the bread would be reduced to a puny piece that barely could sustain me for another day.

Chapter 22:
The Carpentry Shop

Surely my newly learned skill as an electrician will be of use to the Germans wherever they're sending us. If I only didn't waste two years in that dreary carpentry shop. At first it wasn't so bad when I was an office boy and even given a bike to deliver bills to ghetto institutions for their orders of office furniture. Merrily I would pedal away with my bag of bills, attracting envious stares of haggard pedestrians who saw no vehicles in the ghetto except for a few other bike-runners or King Chaim's droshky. I felt important then, and rode through the streets with an air of purpose and urgency. With no telephones in the ghetto, the factory bigwigs had to communicate only by messenger.

But my good job didn't last. Our shop's master foreman, Fuchs, soon appropriated the bike for himself, claiming that only he was important enough to avail of such a rare device. Yet even he had to give up this convenience when the Nazis banned all bikes in the ghetto, even for official use. I had to make my rounds on foot over long, drab streets. But I didn't mope, and walked jauntily, often singing catchy German marching tunes for rhythm. Singing also kept down my awareness of the ever-nagging hunger.

The loss of the bike was soon topped by a worse deprivation: another boy bumped me from the office into the factory; his backing was stronger because his dad, Mr. Kantor, was master-foreman of the huge Holzgalanterie where produced furniture went directly to German administrators of the ghetto, and to the Gestapo, and to the Kripo. I was demoted to a floor-boy in the cold and dusty workshop.

My freedom of movement, when I worked on errands for the office, was over. The cabinet makers would order me to fetch lumber, sweep up the sawdust and shavings from around their benches, and help them assemble larger pieces. When two or more would need me at the same time, they'd all yell and drive me batty. The physical labor was demanding, and I could hardly keep up with those strong carpenters who knew how to use their sinewy arms when moving lumber. The worst errand was when they'd send me down for lumber to the huge machine shop on the main floor. The incessant buzzing and whizzing of electric saws with their enormous circular cutting blades was scary and deafening. Splinters were flying and the air was saturated with sawdust, which got into our eyes, nose and mouth. The men who operated them were in constant danger as they pushed the lumber with their hands close to the whirring blade while the dust blinded them. Once, a machinist lost a few fingers while sawing, yet had to show up for work with his arm in a sling and was assigned to another job. Soon there were more boy-apprentices hired and my strenuous duties eased somewhat. But we were just flunkies, carrying heavy logs to the carpenters' benches, then aid them by holding on to a board while they shaved it, and finally remove the finished pieces of furniture. Yet they were always dour and gruff and not about to impart the secrets of their trade nor even chat with us. They would get paid by piecework and always rushed to finish those long tables, stools and cabinets, then rush us to carry them away to the shipping room.

The immense hall with the workbenches was freezing in winter, and we often gathered around its single stove to shake off the chill. If we were lucky enough to have a raw potato, we'd slice off slivers and put them on the stove, then watch the flakes slowly turn brown as we salivated, inhaling their delicious aroma. Sometimes we'd share these toasted chips with each other and slightly relieve our constant hunger. The warmth of the stove was another delight that I couldn't experience at home where we no longer had anything to burn and where we even shivered under the down comforters. The warm stove and the slightly appeased hunger would make us nod. This infuriated the director of the plant, Mr. Rosenblat, who used to sneak up like a predator on the prowl to catch us being idle and then punish us. If we spotted him in time, we'd run to a work bench of the nearest carpenter and act busy. By the time he left the floor, our precious nourishing chips on the stove, if we had any that day, were burnt and wasted.

The carpenters were paid with extra food rations and didn't suffer such hunger as we did. They would bring pots with coffee or soup from home that they would heat on the stove, often shoving aside our precious toasting chips. The aroma of their home-cooking would spread in the workshop and make our mouths water. Our strongest boy, a strapping sixteen-year-old, named appropriately Cederbaum, or cedar, would try to endear himself to the carpenters and lifted enormous pieces of lumber for them all by himself. But he ultimately injured his spine with one of these feats of strength and died.

Chapter 23:
The Electro-technical Workshop

So, at least now I have a vocation that the Nazis will surely find useful. Leaving that dreary cabinet-making plant was lucky. Now, with more than a year of experience at the electro-technical shop, I can claim to be an electrician. There, sitting with other boys in vocational classes, I also resumed some schooling, which had been denied to Jews four years ago. Occasionally, I would assist an electrician on installations outside the shop, handing him his tools as he stood on the ladder uttering grunts. But I didn't mind being a flunky there because I was acquiring a vocation.

Engineers were the new elite in the ghetto as craftsmen essential to the German industry. Men who could mold metal or control electric currents had a better chance to survive. We considered ourselves lucky to be working as budding electrical and metallurgical engineers. We felt like students in an exclusive learning institution. Another godsend was a daily bowl of soup for us youngsters, which would often be our only meal for the day.

Highly motivated, we would even experiment at home with our new skills. Some even tinkled with radios, forbidden to be owned by Jews under the threat of death. I took a chance on a heating coil, suspending it from a socket in our room at home to keep Mama and me warm. This was considered sabotage because it supposedly diverted power from the German war industry. But fearing punishment and even death for an offense against this prohibition gave way to a more urgent need of self-preservation: to fight off immediate death in our freezing home.

To give our classes legitimacy in case of an unexpected German inspection, the plant's administrators would sponsor them under the guise of vocational training vital for industry. There were about thirty of us teenagers, who gladly flocked to that little room daily from nine in the morning till noon – working hours for adults – where math, algebra, trig, calculus, physics, and electrical and metallurgical engineering were taught. Some pupils had shown great aptitude for scientific study. We were in the charge of Mr. Gustav Kolski, a public school principal in pre-war Lodz. Among those we respected who came up to teach us were Mr. Themes, a metallurgical engineer, and Mr. Fenster, an electrical engineer.

Soon I had learned enough to go alone on a private job to install a new power line for some woman and her daughter, and earned fifteen marks in Rumeks, our ghetto currency, the first of such an earning in my new profession. It wasn't much, but it delighted Mama and thrilled me by giving me a new feeling of self-worth and independence.

Those of us more talented were already calculating the power necessary for recoiling burned-out motors and rotors that had to be salvaged because no new machinery was sent into the ghetto. Motors that would have been junked before the war had to be miraculously restored and put to work again. It was fascinating to watch, as if a new soul was being put into a dead carcass and made it come alive. First, we carefully removed the burnt wiring from the grooves of the motor; disentangled it, straightened it and stripped it from its charred insulation, then buffed it intensely for a couple of hours until the copper regained its shiny gloss. The refurbished wire was sent to another workshop, covered with new insulation and returned to us. Master-engineers calculated the amount of coils needed in the grooves for creating the motor's magnetic fields. Senior technicians rewired it with the newly insulated wire, and – Presto! The engine would come alive, spinning with its original efficiency. Another irony: *everything was done to revive dead machines but nothing to sustain the lives of people dying from hunger!*

The serving of soup for the pupils was a break from class, often an amusing one. It would give us a chance to poke fun at Mr. Kolski, a tall scarecrow of about fifty, with huge owlish eyes set in hollow sockets under bushy eyebrows, and straight black hair streaked with gray always combed back and pasted close to his head. The students had little respect for him because he was merely a general educator, not an engineer. Gussie, as we mockingly called him among ourselves, would make a big production during the soup serving. Instead of having us just stand in line for it, he would call each of us by name to come individually to the front of the class where the kettle would stand near his desk and where the woman from the public kitchen would serve it as if she and Gussie were bestowing some special award to each of us, while he scurried around the kettle, peering worriedly into it every time she would dip the ladle to fill a student's mess tin. Surely he fretted that if her helpings for us were too generous with the thick contents from the bottom, only thin broth would be left for him at the end.

"Just look at Gussie hovering over the kettle like a vulture!" snidely quipped our class clown, Jedwab, as we chuckled and giggled, elated with anticipation of a warm meal. But our helpings were often disappointingly thin because the servers, intimidated by Gussie's busy presence, or perhaps because they felt sorry for the old coot, ladled him the most nourishing solids while leaving the thin stuff at the top for us. "Getting it from the bottom" was also reserved for our instructors who came up during feeding to get theirs.

After the server and the kettle were out, Gussie would sit facing us at his desk and eat his double portion while we hungrily slurped our one scoop. His manner of eating amused us so much that it almost made up for the unfair servings. He'd lift each spoonful and, for a moment, admire its contents as if it were some work of art before he made it disappear in his cavernous mouth. On a chilly day in the unheated classroom, there was more fun. As Gussie was chewing and holding up his next spoonful to admire it solicitously, a big, clear drop of snivel would crystallize at the tip of his pointed nose, quiver and threaten to drop into his mess tin. We whinnied with glee when the ominous globule would finally plop down while he was oblivious to it. Jedwab, ever the comic, would quip: "That's one way to increase your serving," or "Poor Gussie's soup is getting too watery," or "It'll take him forever to finish if he keeps adding on like that," amusing us as much as Gussie's plopping nose droplets. The cold classroom and the hot soup made all our noses red and runny. But our discomfort was eased by the sight of our priggish principal who slurped his soup with a dripping nose. It was good to laugh if only to balance the gravity of our predicament. A class clown like Jedwab was great to have around.

The floor was always abuzz with political discussions by young idealists. The engineers and master electricians kept away; being part of the plant's administration, they were regarded by those boys as "servile flunkies of capitalism" and not true proletarians. Maybe the older workers doubted the sincerity of those young men from mostly middle-class backgrounds who advocated abolition of private property, and denounced their own once prosperous fathers. Maybe they mocked the idealism of these would-be world saviors. Or maybe all this lofty rhetoric and promises of utopias rang hollow to them in view of our dire situation in the grip of the Hitlerites and always on the brink of disaster.

The plant was under the direction of Engineer Weinberg, a genial, polite and easy-going mastermind of all electrical works, not only in the ghetto, but in the entire city of Lodz. The Germans valued him highly and often took him out of the ghetto to locate power problems in the city proper. His pleasant personality and cheerful manner also won him respect and admiration by us all even though, as a factory director, he was an "exploiter of his proletarian laborers." He was about fifty and had a son, Jerzyk, of about twenty, whom he often left in charge. But relations with Jerzyk were often strained. Once they even exploded in a beating of Jerzyk by an angry young "revolutionary".

Jerzyk Weinberg was a dashingly handsome playboy with the looks of an Aryan idol: tall, lanky, with pale blue eyes and a long and narrow aristocratic face topped by a mane of blond, wavy hair, a true model for a Greek sculpture. He carried on a romantic relationship with the plant's nurse, a pretty and voluptuous brunette of about twenty-five, and would often chat with her outside near the infirmary. He greatly resembled his dad who was, however, much shorter and squat. Unlike his dad, Jerzyk had an arrogant and insolent manner about him and would address the workers haughtily, especially the younger ones.

The sixteen-year-old Lolek Aksztein, who thrashed him, was scrawny and much shorter. But he was a feisty, sinewy, street-wise fighter. He didn't like Jerzyk's high-handed manner and, after having some words with him, knocked him down and, sitting astride his chest, kept pounding the handsome face until people pulled him off the Adonis. Yet nothing was done to punish Aksztein. The workers rallied behind him, regarding this conflict as a struggle between the working class and the exploiting capitalism, so the administration decided to disregard the whole incident. The workers' firm stand was also due to Lolek's background as a waif of the street. They were bothered by their own cushy pre-war lives as sons of well-to-do respectable parents and tried to right the wrongs of an unjust and unequal society. Here they saw a poor, smaller and scrawny boy, winning a fight with a bigger and well-fed son of a ghetto bigwig; hence, the downtrodden working masses overcoming the oppressive social system and, in a larger sense, perhaps triumphing over the scourge of Fascism.

Lolek was a son of an abandoned servant girl. He was quite outspoken, and the hopeful young socialists recruited him, probably to give their cause a genuine proletarian aspect. He would spew the usual leftist clichés about blood-sucking bosses who got labor out of workers by exploitation. Yet I hardly ever saw Lolek at work. He was mostly making his rousing speeches and bursting out at opponents; a veritable little Trotsky or Hitler.

These young enthusiasts would sing communist songs about the up-coming victory of the proletariat and the defeat of Fascism. They would denounce the West, which "was decaying because capitalism was rotten to the core." They would laud the Red Army as the only force capable of stopping the Hitler horde that "rose to power as fascist dogs hired by the capitalist West in cahoots with German financiers and industrialist who want to destroy the Soviet Union, which is bringing liberation to the working class."

I, too, would get caught up in the spirit of these tunes because I loved to sing, but this did not grant me acceptance in their secret gather-ings. They probably excluded me as a "rotten petty-bourgeois" because I didn't try to join their heated debates in a corner of the vast main floor. At home, Mama smiled indulgently, pleased that her pampered boy was becoming socially aware. She probably saw herself a proletarian even though she once worked in her own dad's textile mill. Was she aware that a communist future bode doom for Grandpa as an ex-factory owner? But she dismissed the noble intentions of enthusiastic adolescents who "usu-ally abandon them to raise a family when they grow up and find a mate."

Chapter 24:
Mama's Toil

While my job at the electrical plant was relatively easy, Mama would have to walk every day for an hour to the remote plant of Mr. Klugman's Rug Workshop where she weaved carpets for two years. Her previous job weaving straw boots for German soldiers on the Russian front in the Straw Boot Factory wasn't any easier, though she was always upbeat and never complained. But even her two good jobs, first kneading matzah for Passover, then peeling potatoes in a public soup kitchen, didn't save Dad from starving to death.

Life had not been easy for Dora Weintraub, nee Riesenberg. Even before the war, when a middle-class Jewish wife wasn't supposed to work, but instead devote herself to the care of her family, Mama had to work in Grandpa's factory. Three of her five younger sisters married well enough to idle their days away, as well as her two sisters-in-law, Edzia Lenga and Ala Brzezinska. Aunt Asta took bridge lessons and had a governess for her two daughters. Even as an oldest child in a family of nine, Mama had to do household chores and take care of the younger siblings. Short like her dad, she was petit, full-bosomed with long, wavy auburn tresses and deep blue eyes under long lashes and dense brows arched symmetrically over them. She was so strikingly pretty at sixteen that her picture was displayed in the window of a popular photography shop in the city of Lublin where my grandparents lived before moving to Lodz. She must have had many admirers because of that lovely picture; and yet, she finally married Dad at twenty-nine, one year after her next younger sister Asta did and, like most of her sisters – through a matchmaker.

Why so late? I thought. If she was so pretty at sixteen, why didn't anyone suitable ask for her hand then? I'll have to ask her about it later, when we'll be settled after this harrowing trip…, but it's good no one did until she married Dad for I wouldn't be here.

Actually, I know very little about Mama before she brought me into this world except that she liked to sing, act out and dance with a broom while sweeping her parents' flat to the amusement of her siblings.

And this deportation is her reward for all her travails – the drudgery years of factory work, before and during the war, Dad's starvation to death, and her desperate attempts to keep me, her only child, alive by giving up her food portions. Finally, this concluding phase was preceded by hiding out like hunted animals in the last days of the ghetto's existence, the most traumatic of which was two days ago when Mama and I concealed ourselves in the attic during another raid for hidden Jews in our tenement. When two days prior to this the Germans raided the house, we were still with the two resourceful uncles Heniek and Sym who bribed the soldier to leave us alone. But without them, all we could do was crawl into the farthest nook of the stifling attic in the hope that even if a soldier opened the shutter and looked in, he wouldn't detect us. And we had lain sweating in the August heat, with parched mouths, anticipating that dreaded moment and wondering if he would just chase us out into the yard or shoot us outright, as resisting deportation was punishable by death. When the raid ended after some hours, we came out of hiding… yet all this travail was for nothing, for here we are on this cattle train on the road to who-knows-where…

But she's still with me. She's lasted through everything, and I take her presence for granted. I'm safe as long as she's around. A year ago a friend told me in the ghetto that his mom had just died and noted that I still had the comfort of having mine. Sensing perhaps some envy in his remark, I told him with an uneasy foreboding: "At least you know where she's buried and you can visit her grave, but will I be as lucky?" Now I worry, will Mama and I withstand the evil eyes of the unfortunate ones? After all, people are envious, even friends.

Chapter 25:
The Dreadful Selection

"Surrender your children."

"I have to cut off a limb to save the body."

"Give me the sick! In their place, I can salvage the healthy."

"Do you want the whole population to be annihilated?"

Rumek's impassioned speeches in September of 1942 began our most traumatic period in the ghetto, which ended with the Dreadful Selection and the ultimate banishment of sixteen thousand people and the worst mourning time for those whose close relatives were taken away and sent into the unknown.

"We don't feed useless mouths," claimed the Germans, asking for the surrender of twenty-five thousand "unproductive" Jews for deportation, including children under ten, the elderly and the sick. It was a horrid order when Rumek commanded all parents to turn over their little children or else the Germans would deport the parents with them. He spoke in the streets, coaxing, urging, pleading, reminding us that a German order is irrevocable and tried to console us that he had bargained with them and brought their original demand for twenty-five thousand down to only twenty thousand. People cried and prayed, summoning God to witness such an atrocity, bewailing that even the Pharaoh's edict to slay all Jewish first-born males was benign compared to the Hitlerites' demand to "surrender" *all* little children. Even our Almighty reacted to this ghastly edict by instructing Moses to foil Pharaoh's plan, which resulted in the death of the Pharaoh's own first-born son.

The quota was not met and the Germans promptly took over. They declared a *Sperre* (blockade) in which they themselves would weed out the "undesirable elements." This meant the most brutal of actions. SELECTION, the most dreaded word in the ghetto, indicated family break-ups, the tearing away of little children from their mothers' breasts, of elderly parents from their already grown children, evictions of all hospital patients, and the culling of any frail-looking people. With cordons of soldiers and the Jewish Ghetto Police, they sealed off the ghetto block by block. It was a week of pandemonium and extreme heart-wrenching scenes. We weren't told where the deportees were sent. We tried to believe German assurances that they were being sent to a special camp for lighter work, although we expected the worst. If the Hitlerites treated us, able-bodied and productive workers with their utmost harshness and extremely reduced food supply, how would they treat these fragile souls in need of even more tender care than we did?

"Mothers and fathers, give your children up, and I promise you'll live. We must cut off one arm to save the whole body of our people," Rumek kept on urging. That was easy for him to say; he was in his late sixties and never had any children. But even if he did, he'd be exempt from surrendering them, as many of the privileged were. He, the "Champion of Children" had created an orphanage just two years earlier, and cleared the ghetto streets of homeless, barefoot and half-clad waifs trembling in the cold, often swollen from hunger, whining, begging, lamenting, and singing to tug at the hearts of wretched passers-by. And yet, he had ultimately surrendered these rescued orphans to their uncertain fate. We couldn't believe it!

That infamous selection killed the very soul of our Lodz Ghetto Jews. Parents were faced with an agonizing decision – a veritable Judgment Day – if they surrender their little children for deportation, they'll have to live out the rest of their lives feeling like accomplices; if they join their little tots, they'd abandon their older children, reducing their chances to survive. The parents who tried to join their kidnapped tots were brutally torn away from them and forced back.

Some parents remained in their apartments instead of coming to the assembly with their little ones. Some hid their tots under beds, in closets, and behind fake walls, but the Hitlerites, assisted by the Jewish Ghetto Police, came up and searched every apartment, even climbing the highest floors, dragged out the hidden kids and wrested the tots away from their parents. Children screamed in terror as their parents struggled with those who tried to take them away. Some parents chased the trucks into which their children had been tossed, but the Germans shooed them away or even shot them dead. They often shot the resisters or even tossed their little ones out the windows from upper floors, killing them instantly.

These horror stories reached us in the first two days of the Selection even though we were strictly confined to our building at 38 Zgierska Street, the ghetto's largest tenement complex. On the third day, it was our turn to be selected. With an ominous foreboding and trembling in fear, we went down to the courtyard. Older by five years than the limit of ten, I still worried that the Germans would find me too emaciated. I didn't want to part with Mama who, I knew, wouldn't let me go without a struggle and fight like a tigress for her only cub.

The image of the Selection is still so vivid to me that it is as if it were happening right now. The shouting of the Jewish police; the hubbub of the assembling people was suddenly hushed after a piercing scream: "*Achtung!*" to stand at attention. A dead silence fell on all people assembled in rows as we looked to our left. A tall SS officer, in a black uniform and shiny black riding boots, entered to review us. Some Jewish policemen followed him, and gathered the unlucky ones whom he pointed out; they immediately escorted them to the rear of our huge courtyard where trucks were waiting. Those who "passed" the Selection were quickly dispatched to our building's huge entrance-gate. The officer strutted briskly, pointing at people to step out of their row. When he came near me, I drew myself up to attention, looked straight ahead in military fashion. I avoided eye contact for fear of provoking him, yet saw his pale face twisted in a scowl. He promptly strutted past Mama and me, and we were immediately ordered to join the lucky ones filing in the gate. Once inside, Mama and I hugged each other gratefully: We PASSED! We thought we may yet live to see the end of such abominations!

Chapter 26:
Aunt Andzia's Anguish

But once inside the gate, I noticed with dismay that Aunt Andzia and Uncle Ignatz returned only with their older girl, Gizia,
but without Rysia, their cute little eight-year-old who apparently didn't
"pass."

Pop-pop-pop-pop! Rapid reports of gun shots rang out from the
vast courtyard. Aunt Andzia collapsed as if they hit her directly and silently dropped to the concrete floor. With insane eyes, she jabbed all
ten fingernails into her own face, pulling them slowly down her cheeks.
They left long furrows swelling with blood. Her mouth was open for a
scream but no sound came out. It was frightful to look at her misery and
her deranged expression. She surely thought that the SS man's shots – we
could see him firing at someone who was sinking down – were hitting her
precious little Rysia and snuffing out her life. Uncle Ignatz bent over saying something to her, and then ran out of the gateway and back toward
the yard.

I couldn't help her. What comfort could anyone offer? I was horrified as I watched her agony. How could this classy woman mutilate
herself like that? She must have been in excruciating pain after slumping
to this stony floor on her bare knees that she was surely injured, too.
And that frightful, insane look…, she probably wanted to stab those fingernails into the face of that SS brute instead of her own. The gunshot
reports were still reverberating in my ears. Did those shots indeed end the
life of my lovely cousin Rysia?

Aunt Andzia's act of self-mutilation was surely misdirected; if she could scratch the face of that beastly SS officer who tore away her precious daughter, she wouldn't have punished herself for losing little Rysia…

A strange numbing enveloped me. The German onslaught on Jews had never been so explicit as this dreadful selection. I thought I must detach myself from Aunt Andzia's agony to retain my sanity. I must feel nothing. Tragedy that touches others mustn't affect me, or else I, too, may crack up and start tearing at my face or hair just like Aunt Andzia. Or, I thought, I would dash at the German blackguard with my bare hands and also be shot down like a mad dog. I had to bear this atrocity and try to survive. It must come to pass.

Poor dear Aunt Andzia, who watched her two daughters like a hawk and doted over them. Once, in the good old days before the war, she went into shock when she saw two round little balls in Gizia's crotch, thinking that her seven-year-old girl had sprouted a pair of testicles. How we all laughed when they turned out to be a couple of marbles that Gizia put inside her panties. Aunt Andzia's constant worry about the well-being of her two little daughters was realized with little Rysia's capture. Perhaps the thought of Rysia's death drove her to this madness. Adorable little Rysia, the apple of her eye, so pretty and delicate, a fine little chiseled, narrow little nose, full lips, big beautiful eyes that, since the war, rarely smiled or expressed any joy, and full golden-hair tresses that were always neatly combed and tied with a huge bow in front.

But soon we learned that the bullets put an end to someone else's life. For the moment we were relieved. And lo and behold! Uncle Ignatz, who apparently bribed a policeman with something of great value, returned with Rysia whom he rescued by pulling her from the doomed truck where my hapless little cousin, completely mortified, expected the worst. So who was shot? An elderly woman had dared to protest to the SS officer by pulling out some documents to prove that she was the widow of a decorated German World War I veteran. But her fluent German and her husband's meritorious war service didn't stop the SS beast from shooting her point-blank before hundreds of petrified residents in the yard of our vast tenement. Meanwhile the four Lawits evaded a family disaster.

Chapter 27:
The Aftermath

G reatly relieved that Uncle Ignatz somehow rescued little Rysia, we had returned to our flat to find another surprise: Mr. and Mrs. Feder, and their four-year-old son, who occupied the remaining two rooms in the same four-room flat, emerged from the selection unscathed. Apparently, the Feders had holed themselves up in their two rooms, maybe behind a fake wall, and evaded capture. We had hardly ever heard the boy make noises as tots do, even during normal days. We had seen him only once or twice during those four years we shared the flat with them. They had to pass through our room on their way out, but we had rarely seen Mrs. Feder leaving home and never with their little boy.

The Sperre ended after a week. Some sixty people were shot to death during it. Sixteen thousand people, mostly children, the elderly and hospital patients were sent out into the unknown. In the weeks that followed, many parents whose children had been taken away lost their minds. Some committed suicide; others became totally withdrawn. The Jewish Police became even more reviled for their complicity in rounding up the children.

For many weeks, the ghetto was shrouded in a painful silence. Some parents, to keep from going berserk, convinced themselves that their children were still alive and well somewhere; that the Germans couldn't have murdered their precious ones. The few parents who somehow had managed to save their children kept them from public sight. Children were not seen anymore, and the ghetto had grown even eerier in its stillness with its gaunt silhouettes scurrying silently through deserted streets. A dismal gloom had hovered over the ghetto. The very air seemed to have swelled with a silent protest, as if the apparitions of the deported children wafted over us asking: "How could you do it? Why did you let them take us? " Even when we stood in lines for our meager weekly food rations, we couldn't escape the wailings of those bereaved parents who, in their throes of grief, bemoaned the forcible removal of their children. Nothing could be said to console them. Everybody wondered: Why the children? They are an integral part of us, our very life. You take away our children, and you remove our essence, our future, the core of our existence, our hope, our will to go on living. Uncle Ignatz observed: "Not only have the Hitlerites taken away our right to perpetuate life but are also taking the children that we've already brought into this world."

But the Hitlerites saw it differently: no Jewish idlers, including children, would eat German bread. It was, "We lose our children, the German boys at the front, then you Jews lose yours. After all, it was you Jews who engulfed us in this war. So now bear the consequences!" It didn't matter that we paid dearly for "their German bread" with our slave labor. Bearing and nurturing children was not permissible for Jews. Period! The protective Jewish parents, especially the mothers, were being punished for the very thing that they did best: providing devoted care for their children. How could the world stand by idly and silent, we wondered, as thousands of children were torn away from their parents and sent off to who knows where. It seemed as if that horrific week was to be passed over as if nothing ever happened!

Soon after the Selection, Hela Weiss, our pre-war neighbor, met Mama with a ghastly story: In the shipment of used clothing into the ghetto, she identified her mom's blood-spattered overcoat in which the elderly Mrs. Weiss had been deported. Hela, her dad and two sisters, Masha and Topcia, were inconsolable. We, then, had few illusions left.

Yet there had been rumors that some relatives in the ghetto got post-cards from the deportees. We tried to believe those rumors, though many suspected that the Germans spread them to keep us calm while they forced the deportees to write home before killing them. We didn't know what to believe, but kept hoping for the best and even selfishly expected to be fed better with the "undesirables" out and only workers remaining now.

The night after that mass tragedy, a distraught mother ran through the huge yard of our tenement tearing hair out of her head and screaming: "Give me back my children! God Almighty in Heaven, return my children to me! Give me back my Hanele, my Rifkele, my Yosele! Please, oh, please, give them back to me! No one has the right to separate children from their mothers. Not even God! I want my children back!" It had sent a chill through us as it reflected the state of mind bordering on insanity of all of those mothers who were torn from their little children. Mama and I felt it keenly, for it could have been Aunt Andzia running like that if Uncle Ignatz hadn't rescued her precious Rysia.

A few nights after the selection we saw another chilling sight. Like a Biblical prophet, some demented man wandered the courtyards and, whenever he saw a large group of people, he shouted: "God will strike you just as He smote Sodom and Gomorrah, for you stopped caring for your brothers. Your old folks and your children are being taken away, your hospitals are being emptied of patients and all you can think about is – good riddance, now we can breathe easier and the Germans will leave us alone. God will punish you for this." No one had dared to think the unthinkable: that these children were as good as dead. And yet we continued deluding ourselves that the cruel Nazis would treat those deportees with consideration. The thought that we were witnessing mass murder was too shocking: how can any human being harm precious little children so totally dependent on their parents? No! That thought boggled the human mind and that's probably why few gave credence to stories of children being tossed out of windows during that Selection.

Chapter 28:
Farewell Old Lodz

...staccato, staccato, staccato...

The wheels are moving us ever farther from our native city and its bustling streets. We haven't seen good old Lodz in five long years, only its run-down slum, the ghetto. Ah, Lodz, that ideal place, a veritable Garden of Eden where I had a hospitable house to visit on every major street, with loving aunts and uncles and cousins to frolic around with.

Will I ever see my dear home town again? Will it be as friendly without my many relatives and schoolmates? Lodz, or "boat" in Polish, was indeed like a craft that had carried me and my family safely over the calm waters of childhood. When the Germans renamed our Jewish section as Litzmannstadt Ghetto, Lodz, the boat, changed from a happy ocean liner to a Charon's ferry destined for the Netherworld of Hades.

But what a vibrant metropolis it was then, with its teeming humanity, clanging trolleys, honking automobiles, droshkies and lorries clattering on the bumpy cobblestones, horse hoofs clopping on the asphalt, house peddlers hawking their wares insistently, children calling out to each other across the street with their shrill falsettos dominating the clamor and blending with voices of newspaper boys shouting the urgent headlines, parks reverberating with laughter of children, What a cacophony of sounds! A true city music!

"Trading! Trading! Old rags. Old clothes. I'll buy your old clothing! Rags!"

"Knives sharpened! Knives sharpened! Scissors, cleavers sharpened!"

"Glazier! Glazier! Your broken windows repaired on the spot!"

"Bagels! Hot bagels! Straight out of baker's oven. Come and get them while they're hot! Golden, crisp, hot bagels! Five groshy each or three for only ten groshy."

"Broad beans! Chick peas! Hot beans! Hot and tasty. Real good. Peppered beans!"

"Hot blueberry tarts. Delicious! Hot!"

"Pumpkin seeds! Hot, salty pumpkin seeds. Get 'em while they last."

"Ice cream! Ice cream! Delicious ice cream!"

The vendors, often very young, mere tots, had hawked their goods in thin, high, childish voices during the day when they should've been in school. One wondered how they could give out the correct change without the benefits of a formal education. Their pitches had been hard to resist, especially when accompanied by delicious aromas of freshly baked goods, pungent onions or tangy garlic. Ah! The blissful feeling of crunching one's teeth into a hot, crispy, fragrant, shiny, golden bagel spattered with poppy or sesame seeds and salt, and with a hole in the middle of it, huge enough to slip over a wrist like a thick bracelet where it would wait its turn while you were slowly munching on the first bagel. And the tingling sweet-and-sour flavors of long and hot blueberry tarts, or spicy, tangy broad beans, or chickpeas, or roasted crunchy pumpkin seeds, all so tantalizing. And while one was leisurely strolling down the streets and past open grocery stores, there was the quaint fragrance of freshly ground coffee, smoked fish and meats, bay leaf, chocolate, cinnamon, chicory and hundreds of other appetizing aromas.

The noisy courtyards of the tenements had resounded with the pounding of carpets by housewives with huge straw-beaters or by the rat-a-tat of their cleavers hacking meat on wooden boards to grind it into hamburgers, or the tingling scent wafting out of kitchens of chopped onions, garlic and meats roasting for dinner. The ever-present children yelled and cheered while playing hopscotch, tag, hide-and-seek and what-have-you. The Polish street singers belted out their sad torch songs in the middle of courtyards – ballads of passionate or unrequited love tinged with local flavor. Yet their appreciative audience was never disturbed by such anachronisms as canon fire and exploding grenades in the Trojan War. The housemaids in the flats would listened raptly, tossing coins wrapped in paper at the minstrels. And the balladeer would wink at a cute servant girl in a window whenever his lyrics alluded to some lewdness, though his words were never explicit. The maid's pretty face would then turn crimson, and she'd pitch her donation directly at him.

Ah, those exciting evening strolls on the *deptak*, the beaten path of Lodz's bustling downtown, where the main street was widest and the stores most elegant with crowds of pedestrians and bevies of stylish girls and boys sauntering aimlessly. We were not yet old enough to date, but just taking notice of each other. And so we would keep ogling, smiling, flirting and making loud observations to members of our own group that could be heard by the girls. We'd even dare double entendres with sexual innuendos that were lustily enjoyed by the girls who often expounded on these remarks with additional wisecracks, leading to more giggling and laughter. Ah, those trepidations of a young heart when a passerby's eager eyes would flash him a hopeful glance. How exhilarating! How intoxicating!

Even the downside of Lodz can't blur my treasured memories of it: its forest of stacks belching smoke, drab streets lined with long stretches of somber red-brick factory buildings with an infinity of little, barred windows, and that unstoppable, rhythmic clatter of weaving machines, which was heard even on the street. They gave me the jitters. I'd always cross the street and look at those menacing buildings from a safe distance lest they engulf me into their infernal bowels. And that disagreeable odor of boiled cabbage, cauliflower, sauerkraut, tar, horse urine, and smelly gutters ever running alongside the streets and noisily emptying their foul contents into the sewers… Even all this was better than our horrid ghetto. And where are we going now? What's in store for us now?

Chapter 29:
Playmates

The spacious parks of Lodz were proper for play, but far. So I had mostly romped in the yard of our tenement. Mama had frowned on the children of cobblers, tinsmiths, coachmen and porters from whom I could pick up some bad language and manners. Yet children from prosperous apartments didn't play in the courtyard with children from attics or basement flats. And I would sometimes rough-house with Cesiek Scheider, the Polish concierge's son of our tenement. He had a knack for wrestling and horseplay and also enjoyed making loud noises by smashing a hollowed metal pin on a string against a narrow metal tube loaded with gunpowder. The detonations were ear shattering and I couldn't stand them. But Cesiek would drool. For extra fun, he'd raise a leg and release a thunderous fart. Then he'd neigh with relish and look at me to see how his outrageous behavior affected me.

Cesiek was beefy and somewhat paunchy with flaxen hair always closely cropped. His small eyes, which sat deeply in a slightly bloated face above a narrow, turned-up nose, suggested a pig's snout. He liked to bare his fleshy arms by rolling his sleeves all the way up to his shoulders. At the time, he was probably twelve like I was, or a year older. He used to come out of his cellar-flat into the courtyard wielding a slab of bread in one hand and a raw onion in the other, or, more rarely, a piece of greasy sausage, and take huge zesty bites of each while his narrow eyes watched intently for my reaction over his ability to eat raw onions without wincing. Surely he had been showing off how tough he could be. I had already known he was strong because I couldn't free myself from his headlocks when we wrestled. He also had a penchant for head-butting my rib cage, which I found quite painful, while he only brayed with glee. Another favorite of his was to ask me, with a mischievous grin, to pull his finger. When I did, Cesiek would let out a blast of farts and raise his leg, shaking it vigorously until the bursts subsided, often delighting him with their unexpected loudness.

Another boorish boy, a Jewish kid, Dolek Kohn, liked to introduce himself roguishly as Kondolek, which sounded like a little condom. He lived in the next tenement complex. He was older than I and had the street smarts of an adult. Aunt Hela felt uncomfortable whenever he came over to our home, insolently sizing up her fair figure. He rarely participated in our child-play and knowingly scrutinized everything around with an appraising glance. He had to fend for himself, he told me, and was so independent that he usually fed himself with one hardboiled egg a day, which he'd buy for eight groszy. To me, overfed and doted upon, this had sounded odd. I wondered why his parents weren't concerned with his well-being. Weren't Jewish parents supposed to idolize their children?

When he was alive, Dad kept reminding me to have worthy friends: "Make sure they are smarter than you, so you can learn from them." And yet my two intellectual and older second cousins, Julek and Benek Maliniak, espoused ideas that disturbed Mama. It was just days before the war broke out in September 1939 when we visited them to bid them farewell on their way to the Soviet Union. Sitting at the dining room table were their parents, Aaron and Rozia, and also Julek's fiancee, Estusia Rotkel, who, like Julek, was only nineteen. Benek was seventeen. All three were ardent socialists and decided to leave their prosperous parents – Aaron was a partner with his relatives of a large lumber yard on Gdanska Street in Lodz, and Estusia's parents had a fur business on Piotrkowska Street. The three youths had hoped to live as true proletarians building a workers' paradise in the Soviet Union where oppressed minorities lived free of religious bigotry. Great Aunt Rozia was opposed to it, claiming that God always spared the Jews from calamities. But Julek insisted that God and religion were anachronisms and, to prove it, he dramatically walked up to the open window, looked up at the sky as if to challenge God to strike him and loudly announced that God did not exist. I had flinched as if expecting a flash of lightning and a clap of thunder to strike him dead, but nothing happened! Perhaps we had all waited for something extraordinary to happen, but Julek just turned to us with an indulgent smile. Noticing my alarm, he said: "Man has created a convenient mythology that covers everything starting with the soul, heaven, hell and God with whom he can communicate by prayer and whom he can appease through self denial, self castigation and sacrificial offerings." For these three idealists, their flight to the USSR was not so much an escape from Jew-baiting Germans as it was an opportunity to renounce religion as "the opiate of the masses" and live under "the rule of the proletariat." This was a really heavy blow to their observant parents. I had a high respect for Julek's and Benek's intelligence – they taught me how to play chess, read foreign languages on their postage stamp collection (which they left me and I'm now carrying in my knapsack), and understand Hitler's intentions in his lowbrow *Mein Kampf*. But my faith in God could not be shaken. Mama didn't have to worry.

Mama rebuked Julek for "putting unstable ideas in the boy's head," but didn't dwell on it; war and separation was on everyone's mind. Julek probably became an atheist in Italy where he had recently studied chemical engineering. Mama likely regarded his un-Godly ideas as a passing fad of the West, which always exported political trends like anarchism, socialism, Marxism, fascism. But these ideas didn't seem to shake her as much as the doubt in the existence of God. New -isms pass like fads, but God is forever.

Chapter 30:
Faith and Tradition

Mama's piety and faith in God was our family tradition. I have my phylacteries even on this train, although I haven't put them on since I prepared for my never-to-be bar mitzvah. Nor did I attend public prayers in the ghetto, held secretly in rooms known only to the most observant Jews. Did the Hitlerites forbid us to hold religious services out of malice, or were they really afraid that our massive presence in synagogues and our unified prayers could unbalance their success in war?

Grandpa Saul was observant and pious. Mama and her siblings would sometimes eat Polish ham, but out of respect for Grandpa, they never let him know. Ham for us had been a delicacy probably because it was taboo. Otherwise, everything was kept strictly kosher. He led an austere life, ran his mill, and had devoted his time at home to daily prayers that he recited mostly from memory. He didn't go to the movies, and I don't remember him enjoying any recreation except for playing checkers with me, which for him was a breather from business problems and for me from school assignments.

Observant Jews like him intentionally inflicted physical flaws upon themselves to evade conscription. I surmised this from Dad's funny stories about Jews and Poles who tried to deceive Tsarist recruiters. Some shrewd peasants feigned deafness, others gnarled their fingers and so on. But in the end they were all exposed and got drafted anyway; only those with genuine flaws like damaged eyesight, missing teeth – necessary for chewing the hard-crusted army bread – were let go. I wondered if Dad was rejected because he had a denture for missing upper teeth and

Grandpa for his bad eye that was always covered with dark glasses, which likely had been scarred to keep him out of the Tsar's army.

Saul Avner Riesenberg was quiet, composed, prudent and never raised his voice. People regarded him as good-hearted, honest and reliable. He was squat and shorter than Grandma, wore a beard, and because of his dark glasses some people called him Blind Saul. Grandpa came from a large family in his native shtetl, Czajkowice, and was a self-made man even though he didn't have any formal schooling. Yet, he spoke Polish well. He was lured to Lodz with its sprouting textile industry after World War I and had established himself as a textile manufacturer with a mechanical weaving mill on the ground floor of the sprawling complex of similar factories at 66 Wolczanska Street. Grandpa's plant had provided a comfortable life and had helped him to marry off all his children to carefully selected mates from good families with solid financial backgrounds.

Grandpa's daily praying at home once led to a funny misunderstanding by our Polish maid. There was a tall grandfather clock in our dining room that rang out every hour and that Grandpa scrupulously wound up every few days. Wearing his tallit and phylacteries to recite the daily prayers, Grandpa always had to face the East, the wall against which stood that imposing clock. Our next-door neighbors at 63 Wolczanska Street, the Kaufmans, told us that our maid had divulged "a great secret" to their maid: "My Master is praying to a grandfather clock." We all had a good laugh over it since it showed us how little understanding of religious practices there was between Jews and gentiles in Poland, even between people who shared the same living quarters.

Sabbaths and holidays were celebrated in the large dining room with Grandma in charge of cooking and serving. First, we attended services in the most imposing synagogue in Lodz, on Kosciuszko Boulevard, where we had diligently prayed and listened to the angelic choir of boys' sopranos and the cantor's powerful tenor. It all sounded beautiful and solemn. Surely God and His angels listened to *this* part of the service. As I would sit there, rapt, a blissful peace enveloped me. The inspired singing would fill me with a belief that angels watched from heaven, delighting in these pleadings and glorification of our Almighty. God had it all under control in His orderly universe. Just sitting in that grandiose synagogue in our holiday finery would fill me with joy of communicating with Him personally. Uttering the cryptic, ancient Hebrew words of praise and gratitude for the Universe that He created for us, and promising to obey all His Commandments with charity to all, I had felt assured that I'd be granted long life in health, peace and prosperity.

And later, as we, the males, would walk home from the synagogue – the women had left earlier to prepare the meal – the world was beautiful. The immediate reward for our piety was a sumptuous holiday meal in my grandparent's spacious apartment, where the table would already be lengthened and set with holiday dishes. Sometimes, before the holidays, a live goose was tied by its foot in the kitchen where Grandma would fatten it for a few days. Sometimes a huge carp swam in the bathtub filled with water, and I would see it later scaled on a wooden board by Grandma or Mama. I kept away from the preparations in the kitchen.

When all were seated, Grandma would light candles in a silver candelabra and wave the flames toward her face while muttering prayers. Grandpa would say grace, take a sip of wine from a silver goblet, pick up a huge challah, say a blessing before cutting into it, and slice pieces for everyone. And then we would eat. Ah, the food! Delicious herring bits in oil, garnished with onions, chopped liver, or pickled jelly made of calf feet for appetizers. Then would come the soup. Chicken soup was my favorite if it had a few small, yellow, undeveloped eggs in it. Then, no…, no, I mustn't think about it because it just stirs up my hunger. With the solemnity, the festivity, the aromas and tastes of delicious dishes, and the reassuring presence of so many loving relatives, I felt that we were truly blessed because we were so devoted to God, to His Torah, and were so kind to others.

When I saw Grandpa's revered synagogue on Kosciuszko Boulevard set ablaze just a couple of months after the Germans entered Lodz, I was relieved that he had left earlier for his native shtetl and was spared the sight of such desecration. This impressive structure, erected in the early thirties at an enormous cost to the Jewish community, went up in flames in full view of terrified Jews. Firemen didn't even try to put out the fire, but just kept it from spreading to adjacent houses. Walking by its smoldering ruins on November 14, 1939, I mused that yesterday had been my thirteenth birthday, and I would have been celebrating my bar mitzvah there. I was waiting for God to smite the cheering Germans in a truly Biblical fashion. But He showed no sign of indignation at such sacrilege – not even a November drizzle to smother the flames. This wasn't a crime against us anymore, but against Him! The Nazis were challenging Him, like the Pharaoh once did. Where was the display of His wrath, His might? Where *was* He? Where was a Moses, a Samson, a Judah the Maccabee, a Simeon Bar Kochba? No one was allowed in to rescue the precious Torah scrolls as our synagogue burnt to the ground with everything in it.

The Germans blamed their desecration on the Poles to stir up hatred between us; a few days later they shocked the Poles in turn, by blowing up the monument of Kosciuszko. Then they published a note in the *Berliner Tageblatt* newspaper, that Jews were destroying Polish monuments for which Poles, in retaliation, would burn Jewish synagogues.

Everybody was sad to see Grandpa leave Lodz and his factory. Only a temporary German trustee/executor, a *Treuhendler*, had the right to be in charge of a Jewish-owned factory. Therefore, Grandpa promptly appointed his own employee, an ethnic German foreman. But once the Jewish owners handed over their mills, they were barred from entering them so he had lost control of it anyway. To veil outright appropriation, the Nazis used this procedure in their eventual takeover of Jewish factories. According to Hitler, the Jews enriched themselves only by illegal or unfair exploitation of Christian labor. And so, after all those hard years that Grandpa spent on establishing an honest and productive livelihood and a name for himself, he was completely robbed of it.

The last I remember of Grandpa is his approving look when he saw me absorbed in a bulky tome of *Asch's Polish Dictionary*. Obviously, he was pleased with my efforts to educate myself while schools were closed due to the outbreak of war. His quiet gentility endeared him to me greatly. He never berated me for goofing off, though I felt that he sincerely wished me success in studies. I miss him dearly and probably will never see him again. He subsidized my pricey private school, watching my academic progress, which was probably more important to him than my impending bar mitzvah because he never checked how well I had prepared for it. Maybe he realized that his world was changing and that religion was retreating before a progressive education, and that a youngster in a big city needed to learn more secular things than a boy in a shtetl like where he had grown up.

Dad and Grandpa regarded the synagogue practically as their second home. Surely our Merciful God will act now and protect us from this evil so that we can sustain our everlasting trust in Him on our fateful arrival, wherever it may be.

Chapter 31:
Boyish Fascinations

...staccato, staccato, staccato...
...the ghetto, the ghetto, the ghetto...

If not for these dreadful ghetto years, my teens would have been the most exciting part of my life – the passage of childhood into boyhood and the unveiling of that great mystery – to be in love with a pretty girl who'd return it so that nothing else in the world could matter. The starving ghetto years were not conducive to sexual awakening. I didn't even notice girls unless other boys called my attention to them as with the pretty and sexy fifteen-year-old Irka Schuster, the major attraction in the Electro-technical Workshop. She lived behind it, often basking in the sun on her deck chair in a scanty bathing suit and surely aware of the stir she caused among the boys who always peered at her. We ogled her supple, curvaceous body and that wholesome Shirley Temple face that already knew how to put on a seductive expression. Some of the older boys flirted with her. I just stared longingly, thinking that this part of my life would have to wait for happier times.

And yet, before the war, already at twelve, I was aware of girls and looked at them appreciatively when our volleyball school team played theirs under the sunny June skies. Ah, those willowy twelve- and thirteen-year-old girls with lively, intelligent faces, flaunting their already tanned, shapely bodies in stylish sporting outfits. They were fiercely competitive, leaping high for their smashes while revealing those smooth calves, long limbs and budding buttocks. I regarded those perky bottoms with a sudden awareness of the feminine form. It wasn't lust, but a kind of natural affinity for the female anatomy that was now flickering, flashing and glittering invitingly right before me. And they were already well aware of their sexuality as they cast those furtive glances at our better-looking boys in an atmosphere flush with anticipation. I would get heartthrobs just looking into a girl's pretty eyes set in a cute face that radiated a lively intelligence and playfulness, especially if it was enhanced by a shapely figure. It would all arouse in me a twinge of blissful longing. The future was so full of promise. Just those strange expectations filled me with wonder of how beautiful life could be.

But these feelings have ceased since the age of twelve. All that's left is my first and only erotic dream about the ample-breasted and docile twelve-year-old tinsmith's daughter, Luba, who lived below us in the basement and sometimes played innocent children-games in the yard with us. Now, on this train, I'm seventeen and still innocent.

Another image, a real one, is etched in my mind: I was about seven and on summer vacation in the country, walking along a deserted stretch of shore alongside a stream. The air was full of earthly smells of blooming linden trees, clover, cow manure and stagnant water – an intoxicating mixture of life and nature. Walking alongside was my beautiful Aunt Hela with her friend, Hela Brodt, both bare-breasted and proudly bearing their shapely ample bosoms crested with large, brown nipples. Both were in their mid-teens, blond and tanned. They looked like typical robust Polish farm girls, radiating their loveliness, wholesomeness and youthful insouciance. They treaded lightly, rising up on their toes as if about to soar. Their round, ripe breasts bounced slightly with each stride and were a joy to behold, even though I was still too young to fully appreciate their allure. I was just merrily treading beside them. They were so carefree that they didn't even fear the bees and wasps buzzing about. They were in total harmony with the budding nature. I felt elated walking with them as if I, too, was part of the glorious, fragrant scene humming with life in a true symphony of sounds, shapes and scents.

I wonder if Hela Brodt, with her typical Polish farm-girl looks, is "passing" on the "Aryan side" right now.

Aunt Hela's nose wasn't as snub as Hela Brodt's and she often pushed its tip up. But "Aryan looks" were of no use in the ghetto anyway; once someone had been identified and branded as a Jew, there was no way out of it.

Three days ago, I spent some pleasant moments with Tosia Granek, a lovely, willowy blond, seventeen like me. The two of us ventured to "organize" some food and raided the abandoned private garden of King

Rumek, where we were lucky enough to dig up a couple of potatoes missed by previous raiders. Tosia's clean-cut looks and daring had reminded me of those tanned beauties playing volleyball five years ago.

There were many girls like Tosia who could evoke a fellow's admiration in the Ghetto High School formed in 1940. Teens were pooled into this single learning center in the Marysin section of the ghetto. But the Germans soon engaged all school-age children in the production of goods for their war. As long as it lasted, it was an exciting time to continue learning in the company of girls because, before the war, none of the Jewish schools were coed. It was nice to see how easily boys and girls drifted toward each other, forming groups or couples, and I wondered which girl was destined and waiting for me. But those musings had to be postponed for normal times.

Chapter 32:
Premonitions

...staccato, staccato, staccato...

It's getting lighter in the cattle-car. I'm exhausted from this sleepless night and from recollecting my past. What's ahead? Work in our trades or clearing rubble in Germany? Mama is quiet, surely awake and thinking. Some women whimper, "An evil is awaiting us. Woe is me! God have mercy on us." What if their prediction is right and the Hitlerites lied to us? And what about Mama's moment of vision yesterday when she shattered a mirror while packing, then froze petrified with foreboding? Was she merely superstitious or did she experience a premonition of doom?

And there was Mama's aunt, Rozia, who had a terrifying nightmare three years ago when she woke up with a piercing scream: "A bullet in his head! They killed my Aaron. My dear Aaron. A bullet, a bullet in his head!" She sat up in her bed perspiring and stubbornly repeating that phrase as if she had a real vision and not just a nightmare. In vain, Mama and Dad tried to calm her down, assuring her that it was only a bad dream caused by two failed attempts to escape the ghetto together with Aaron. Was her vision clairvoyance or just stress? Maybe Aaron's spirit actually communicated with her at the precise moment of his leaving this world. She died two years later after a gall-bladder surgery and never did find out, nor did we, if her vision of Aaron's shooting was a fact.

An odd premonition kept me from entering a mammoth cave with my aunts and uncles one summer when I was about seven. Petrified at the gaping dark entrance, I stubbornly refused to go in with the others, who finally went in and left me outside. Could this have been a child's fear of dark places or a foresight – the total disappearance of all my relatives for their daring to invade the entrails of a forbidden sanctuary?

An odd foreboding also spared me from a likely doom when I was about five. I insisted on sleeping in my parents' bedroom one night. Somebody forgot to turn off the gas on the kitchen range that night and our two girl lodgers who roomed next to it fell unconscious and were taken to a hospital. My bed in the living room was closer to the kitchen than my parents' bedroom, and had I slept in it as usual, I would have probably died.

And two days ago, my twelve-year-old cousin Lilka baffled me with what could have been her clairvoyance. Her puzzling gaze still haunts me. We were alone while the adults were out, probably looking for food or checking on our prospects of going into hiding if the deportation continued. We kept hoping that they would stop when the insatiable Hitler-Moloch was finally gutted with deportees. As the two of us sat on the floor on some mattresses among packed suitcases, bundles and knapsacks, Lilka's usually cheerful and carefree expression was replaced by a pensive, quizzical half smile; even her cute nose, which earned her the nickname *Mopsik* or little pug dog, didn't seem as funny; her round, cherubic face adorned by straight dark bangs, was almost serious. Her blithe, brown eyes were earnest, wistful, expectant, staring at me without their familiar mischievousness. I felt perplexed. How was I supposed to react? I was dismayed at my own confusion and Lilka's misty eyes and forlorn gaze. Surely, she had more experience than I, if only from observing her older sister's trysts (I once espied saucy Stefa on the sofa with a handsome young man when I visited them unexpectedly). Lilka's gaze at me was too deliberate for a girl her age. Was she also experiencing a premonition of impending doom and trying to challenge me to do something that would initiate us into the loss of our innocence just in case we never reach adulthood? But I didn't know anything about *that*! I'm seventeen, but inexperienced, even ignorant. I've never even kissed a girl. Before the war, I got close to them on occasions and felt the eager stirrings of manhood, but that's all. My sex urge must have been stunted due to years of extreme hunger. Besides, Lilka was just a little girl, not even developed. Surely I misread her intentions! But her strange look had suggested an opportunity to do the yet unknown. A test of my manhood. But how?! Surely not there! And not with her!

Not knowing how to react, I did nothing and pretended not to draw any conclusions from her gaze. Now she's on her way to God knows where. Like her sister, she had that insatiable lust for life and wanted probably to experience sex even if it had to be with a first cousin. Was I right not to respond to her challenge, depriving her of a last wish? But what if I had misread her expression and made a pass at her and she accused me of being vile? Or what if her parents had suddenly entered the room and caught us? They'd never forgive me. I'd be disgraced. But even if she had welcomed my advances, what did I know? It would have just been an experiment. But then, maybe, that's all she had wanted. Even if the experience didn't turn out to be pleasant, she'd have at least gained knowledge of that secret before her untimely…, no, no! It can't be! I mustn't think of *that*! She'll still learn all about life in due time. This can't be our last road. Even though my past is fleeting by with all these vivid images, I can't see my own mortality. Not at seventeen. Not when I feel my whole life is still before me, challenging me, and little Lilka as well. Please, God, let her have many chances to find the right boy in due time so that she can discover that secret adult experience in relaxation and not under the threat of it being her last experience on this earth.

Part II:

Welcome to Murderopolis

Chapter 1:
Raus! (Out!)

The train is slowing down. At last we may be pulling into a station. The cattle-car is filled with daylight now. Anxious to know what's on the outside, we shout questions at the few tall men who are peering through the little barred porthole near the ceiling. The dragon train is now at a crawl. The clanging of switches or brakes indicates that we're pulling into a sizable depot. A stop, a yank. A thud of the couplings. It halts. A wrench, a jerk. Those who got up topple on each other. I get up and push myself through to have a glimpse outside. Luckily, I'm tall enough to look out, but only when I stand on my tiptoes. There's another cattle-car train on the tracks next to ours. It's probably moving, but it's hard to tell because ours may still be in motion.

A strange sight unfolds before me: Behind the little barred window of the other train, men stand in striped blue-and-white caps on shaven heads, wearing identical blue-and-white striped jackets. It seems their faces are petrified with pain. One, who is near the opening, stares at me silently and bears a mournful expression on his gaunt and familiar-looking face. Perhaps he arrived from our ghetto earlier and has already been processed. But his silence and grave look are alarming. The men standing next to me shout to him loudly: "Where are you from? Where are they sending you? What kind of station is it? Where are they going to send us?" But he and the others are mum. No response whatsoever. It is as if they can't hear us at all. It seems they can easily answer because both trains are alongside each other. And yet, they silently keep looking at our agitated faces. Don't they have any compassion for our anxiety? I see a fleeting glimpse of pity on the face of the man standing next to the window.

Suddenly – a screech, a clang – the train comes to a dead stop. Those of us on our feet lose balance and topple over those sitting on the floor. Screams of disgust rise from those near the vat, that splatters them with its repulsive contents. The tumult intensifies as a grinding clank of metal latches signals the unbolting of doors in the adjoining cars.

"*Raus! Raus! Schnell! Los!* (Out! Out! Fast! Move!)" A crescendo of voices, shrill and grating, urges people to exit. Gone is the customary and congenial "*Aussteigen*" announcement to disembark typically used by German railroad officials. In the absence of this civilized formality, the "*Raus*", barked with a furious frenzy in strident voices, sounds even harsher – though it's probably fitting for passengers arriving in cattle-cars instead of Pullmans, I suppose.

A loud clang of the bolts and hasps now signals the unlocking of our boxcar. The door is flung open with a jarring clash of metal. An equally metallic shriek rings out, piercing through all other noises: "*Raus! Alle raus! Los! Schnell! Rrraus!* (Out! All out! Move! Fast! Out!)"

The people piled on the floor of our overcrowded car are too numbed from long hours of being cramped to react instantly. The shrill tone of the "*Raus*" chills us to the bone. It is commanding, mandatory, absolute. There isn't one shred of humanity in it. Circus animals could perhaps be addressed in this way. It's ruthless, relentless, sinister and gushes hatred. It's a screech borne in hell and it dwarfs us with its evil foreboding.

"*Raus! Raus! Raus! Schnell! RRRRAUS!!!* (Out! Out! Out! Fast! OOOUT!!!)" The intensity of that blood-curdling word is at its highest pitch. It's replete with an escalating urgency. It reverberates with menace. It penetrates the mind, leaving an indelible stamp like a gong in hell heralding eternal damnation for its wretched inhabitants.

We are numb, frozen with fear. Our aching limbs refuse to move. The SS and their striped flunkies reach in and grab the people closest to the door. They drag them out by their clothes like sacks of potatoes. They jerk them down, tossing them on top of those who already tumbled down. The voices ring out again, ferocious, hysterical, in the highest register: "*RRRRRRAUSSS!!!*"

They're lashing us with this hideous word and its contemptuous tone. They prolong the final "s" which comes out like the hiss of a roused serpent. They growl it at us with its rolled "r" – a guttural sound in German – which the blusterers first gurgle in their throats like snarling dogs, than snap out like a vicious bark: "*RRRRRRAUSSS!!!*"

We are stupefied from the eerie night, mangled from the painful positions on the floor, chilled to the bone by these harsh, frenzied barks that whip us into a delirium of terror. "*RRRRRRAUSSS!!!*" blares the infernal word as if welcoming us to the gates of hell. Some people are so terrified they lose control of their bowels, which is clearly audible. This and the vat filled to its brim with excrement add to a stifling stench. The car smells like a cesspool, and yet the people are balking to step out into fresh air. We are petrified.

"*RRRRRRAUSSS!!!*" The commands electrify us with their urgency. A few husky men in the same blue/white stripes now hop into our car and start tossing the reluctant people out. They must be some special crew in the service of the SS that'll process us during our temporary stay at this station and on our way to work in Germany. They swiftly bustle the passengers and show familiarity with their duties even without waiting for the commands of the SS men. Obviously, they've been handling such transports as ours many times before. "Leave your bundles on the train," they tell us reassuringly in Yiddish. "You'll get them later." I know that the Germans are very orderly and organized, but how will we be able to retrieve our own bundles in all this messy detraining?

"*RRRRRRAUSSS!!! Alle raus! Los! Schnell!* (OOUUT!!! All Out! Move! Fast!)*" Agitated, feverish, horrified, our people grab their bundles and rush toward the door pushing, shoving, tripping, falling over each other. They spill out of our jam-packed cattle-car and scurry onto the platform, bewildered, while the German officers outside are calm and collected and stand there regally as if posing for a portrait, half bored and half amused at the pandemonium.

How will these thousands of bundles left in the wagons ever be found and claimed by their rightful owners, one wonders. They contain the most important personal articles of peoples' lives, the only ones they still deemed worthy of bringing. Some people won't part with their bundles and try to get back into the car to retrieve them, but they are brutally beaten. This dissuades others with similar intentions. An SS man holds a man by his collar while another SS man delivers crushing blows with a rifle butt to the man's rib cage. The man groans with each thud, but doesn't protest.

I still stand with Mama in the back of the car lest we get trampled in the stampede for the exit. Since no one is crowding the little window anymore, I get near it to take another glimpse out. The train that moved on the other tracks is now gone. Beyond, I see a huge, rocky field and a group of men in vertical blue/white zebra-striped uniforms and matching round caps without visors loading or unloading rocks from wheelbarrows and lorries. Not far from them and nearer to our train, I notice a squat SS officer just as he picks up a huge, jagged rock and hurls it at the men working in some distance. As the rock is about to strike them, they deftly dodge it without turning around. I'm amazed at their alertness. The rock could have crushed their bones if it found its mark. Apparently, they were watching the SS man without even looking at him. As if they had eyes in their backs. I quickly look at the SS man to catch his reaction of likely disappointment. But he's laughing. He's not angry at missing his mark. I look at the prisoners again. They, too, are laughing as if in admiration of the SS man's strength and accuracy. It's like a game. Still laughing, the officer shouts: "*Feierabend!* (Knock off work!)", signaling a break for the men. So the whole incident is just good-natured fun, unless, of course, one of the men, not quick enough to dodge, gets injured. Will the German, then, get even more cheerful or more upset that one of his work-crew lies bleeding and hurt, a clumsy loser in a clever game of skill and alertness devised by this fun-loving, squat SS officer?

Our wagon is nearly empty now. The giant dragon-train is spewing out people like droppings from its cavernous, malodorous boxcars. We finally jump out on the platform while desperately trying to hold on to our dearest ones and to our bundles. To the SS brass standing in small groups at some distance, aloof, imperious, exalted and seemingly unconcerned with all the hubbub and confusion – to them we must indeed look like so many turds belched out from this infernal train. Or perhaps, that's what they, in all their Aryan splendor, wish to see – Jews as a subhuman species, a disposable refuse, a trainload of smelly livestock shipped on schedule for its routine processing. In the grand scheme of things, we must fit the image concocted by their exalted Fuehrer and his propaganda machine. Meanwhile, they're posing as veritable supermen, tall, erect, stiff-necked, in German military fashion, in shiny black riding boots and spiffy uniforms. Some officers chat amiably with each other, wholly unconcerned with our plight. Some appear bored, their eyes looking over and above us like generals scanning a distant battlefield while leaving the handling of minor details, such as us, to their underlings and to zebra-striped prisoners. The detached demeanor of the high brass contrasts with the rampant savagery of the soldiers, who, with their guns-at-the-ready, bark orders and whack people.

The husky zebras keep urging us in Yiddish: "Don't worry about your belongings. Don't look for them now. You'll get them later. Just line up for processing. Men and women separately. Go to the right column!"

"*Los! Los! Schnell! Los!* (Move! Move! Fast! Move!)" They shout orders in Polish, German and Yiddish, shoving the disoriented people into a column formation. "Five abreast. Form a column! Fast! Fast! Five abreast!"

The zebras are aided by the SS men who rush us with their rifle butts and furiously keep hitting people right and left as if they were on a battlefield in a hand-to-hand combat. There's bedlam. Distraught mothers are tightly holding their little children who sense their mom's trepidation and are horrified. In the bustle, relatives lose sight of each other and try to find them by searching the already-formed ranks and by calling out names of children or parents. "Mommy, Mommy! Daddy!"

I suddenly realize that I'm going to be separated from Mama. The thought is too dreadful to consider: to lose each other now after we've already been separated from all her sisters and their husbands. And the Germans promised that families would *not* be separated. This is an awful fate for me and her, but in the rush of things, I don't have any time to dwell on it. I give Mama a hasty kiss. She tries to prolong the embrace, but I break away quickly to save us from the brutal intrusion of an SS man's rifle butt.

I join a column of men. Convulsively, I hold on to my knapsack with its contents and, most important of all, our cherished family photos. Mama enters the row of a women's column that is alongside the men's. She's also carrying a bundle. Now I'll also be without a mother. My adolescent urge to be independent from parental supervision has materialized at last. But at what price! Knowing that she'll be in the hands of these brutes, that she may be harmed, that her very life may be threatened – it's ghastly to think it.

Herded along the ramp on the left side of our train, we wait for "processing". We stretch our necks to see what's going on at the head of our column. Around us, the SS men are hitting lingerers and shoving them into formation. Some people moan and bleed from gashes to the head. Some youngsters push their way back toward the rear, probably to avoid or postpone the inevitable. We're stretching our necks to see the front of our long column. What's going on at the head of it? What are we waiting for?

Soon we know. As we inch forward, I see some SS officers at the head, one of whom selects the new arrivals. He's flanked by SS men with rifles at the ready to make sure that those selected join their assigned ranks. If someone doesn't, then they hit him or her with their rifles and kick them mercilessly. Obviously, the selection here is just a repeat of those dreaded selections in our ghetto, where those who were unable to work were weeded out and shipped into the unknown. Children under fourteen and older people, or those too skinny, feeble or infirm, are sent to one group; those physically fit are sent to another. Surely the Germans won't do the frail group any harm, I reason, as we all did in the ghetto. They'll probably send them into another camp where they'll be given less food and live in more uncomfortable and crowded dwellings.

I'm trying to see Mama in the women's column next to us. I am not sure if I'll ever see her again. But I push that thought away. My attention is drawn to a young woman who is skinny and very pale, with eyes distended in fear, and who frantically applies some kind of rouge to her pale, hollow cheeks. She pinches and slaps her own face until it flushes and reddens. But it's an unhealthy color, bricky rather than pinkish, and no better than her sickly pallor. Another woman in that column, a faded blond beauty in her fifties, holds a small mirror trying to apply lipstick, but her trembling fingers keep smearing it all around her lips. Will her statuesque appearance spare her from being sent to the "junk heap"?

Chapter 2:
A King Deposed

As our column inches forwards, a new sight catches my eye. Our King Rumek walks over to a group of SS officers on the side, some of whom are viewing the goings-on. He draws himself up, clicks his heels in German military fashion, which looks ridiculous for this bent, gray-haired civilian in his sixties, and shouts out: "*Ich melde gehorchsam dass ich bin der Aelteste der Juden von* Litzmanstadt Ghetto, *und das hier ist meine Familie.* (I'm dutifully reporting that I'm the Eldest of the Jews of Litzmannstadt Ghetto, and this here is my family.)" He points to the back of him, where at a respectful distance, stands his much younger, pretty wife and his brother with his own wife. All three are facing the German brass in hopeful anticipation. For a second my heart leaps up. Yes, yes, let them know who you are, I root for him silently, indeed who we all are – hard-working people of the ghetto who slaved and starved for four and a half years so that the German soldiers were well clad.

But as I glimpse at the SS brass for their reaction to Rumkowski, my heart sinks. His flowing white hair and military report made no impact. Their faces and demeanor ooze disdain. Some sneer. Some continue staring dramatically into the distance not the least concerned about our King, or of the horrific scenes taking place on the platform. Some bear expressions of veiled mockery or gloating malice. Our exalted ruler is swiftly becoming a has-been. He's not finding much sympathy in here. My hope quickly deflates. Mama and I showed up for this transport voluntarily mainly because we knew that Rumkowski himself was going to be on it also. His imposing presence was our most reliable assurance that the whole ghetto was indeed being relocated to Germany as a tactical retreat from the approaching front – just as the Germans claimed.

One of the SS officers, with an expression of restrained mockery, looks him over slowly, then his three relatives, and answers with a feigned deference: "Yeah, you can stand right here, and we'll soon provide you all with special transportation as befits the Eldest of the Jews and his family." He turns to the other SS officers, to note their reaction, then, with repressed hilarity, roars to the scurrying zebras: "*Los! Schnell!* Provide special transportation for the Eldest of the Jews of Litzmannstadt Ghetto!"

Now the SS men have a ball at King Rumek's expense. Obviously they're enjoying this unexpected comic interval in their routine task of separating grieving families. This elderly, bespectacled Jew, with an imposing white mane, dares to petition these high-ranking *Uebermenschen* (supermen) for special consideration. Privileges!?! At a selection where either eyeglasses or white hair alone are enough to qualify a Jew for the "junk heap"?! Poor King Chaim the First. Five years ago, the Germans appointed him to the grim task of running the ghetto packed with over two-hundred thousand people. And they bestowed on him the impressive title as the Eldest of the Jews. Perhaps they picked him because his hooked nose, dark-rimmed glasses, and white mane fit their stereotype of a powerful, scheming Jew straight out of the pages of *Der Stuermer* or *The Protocols of the Eldest of Zion*. But his faithful servitude earned him neither respect nor gratitude now.

Many of the ghetto Jews, particularly those who were forced to give up their children in the dreadful selection of 1942, accused him of collaboration with the Hitlerites. He did what he had to do on their orders and probably, along with the rest of us, hoped for the best and for their civility. Now I feel sorry for him and am dismayed at his humiliation. For five long years, he was revered by many ghetto Jews, glorified by artists, painters and poets with his visage emblazoned on ghetto currency and all official publications. He rode his droshky through the ghetto like a king in his coach – the horse being the only animal in the whole ghetto. He made long impassioned speeches on matters of life and death to the thousands of us – his captive subjects. But the scornful reception of the SS brass here bodes him no good.

My column is moving forward. I rise on my tiptoes to get a glimpse at the goings-on in front. One officer selects men in our column and another selects the women in their column, sending them either to the right or to the left. The people around me are frantically trying to look their very best. Their trepidation is now getting to me, too. I must lie and say that I'm eighteen years of age even though I still have a few months left to go. I'm drawing myself up, push out my chest, and suck in my emaciated gut. "*Ich bin achtzehn Jahre alt,* (I'm eighteen years old,)" I repeat to myself in German, trying to get it out as snappily as I can.

Suddenly, on my left, I see a dilapidated cart being pulled with Rumkowski standing in it forlornly with his brother and both their wives. I glance toward the SS brass that he approached earlier and see them doubled up in laughter. Indeed King Chaim the First presents a sorry sight as he tries to keep his balance on that shaky nag-drawn country crate. Who knows what else he'll have to endure as their laughingstock?

What will they do with him? What's awaiting us all?

Chapter 3:
Passing the Selection

"*Ich bin achtzehn; Ich bin achtzehn*, (I am eighteen; I am eighteen)," I'm frantically repeating to myself as I get near the selecting officers. I'm afraid to breathe lest my puffed-up chest deflates. I now see the SS officer clearly in his well-tailored uniform and shiny black riding boots as he points his finger in a white glove negligently, with just a flick, either to the left or to the right, his implacable face seemingly bored by the tedium of his repetitive task. Flick! – goes the finger, slashing through the air like a falling guillotine. Flick! – goes the fateful finger like a magic wand to the other side. Why the white gloves? Is he distancing himself from this sordid selection a la Pontius Pilate's symbolic hand-washing for crucifying Jesus?

He questions some people. I can't hear what he asks, perhaps their age or profession. I'm too busy preparing my own answer if he asks for my age. "*Ich bin achtzehn*," I repeat again and again to get it out flawlessly. I stand on my toes to also appear taller, even though I'm already tall. "*Ich bin achtzehn*," I recite like a prayer, hoping that this phrase with its magic number will be my ticket to work, as the letters that stand for eighteen also read *life* in Hebrew. The officer will see that, as an adult, I'm fully able to do a man's job. "*Ich bin schon achtzehn Jahre alt*. (I am already eighteen years old.)" I keep embellishing my phrase with extra words in the hopes of impressing him with my command of German, which may also sway his momentous decision. But in my fluster I fumble them, changing their order, and can't get them out smoothly enough. I begin to curse the guttural German language with its speakers, although four years ago in school I learned to appreciate its structure, its flow and its idiom.

But my agitation is futile because the officer doesn't waste any time on questioning me. Without batting an eyelash, his face oozing indifference, his finger flicks, and I, without even knowing if it bodes me good or bad, step briskly to my newly assigned column. To my great relief I'm now with the "able-bodied". I can breathe easier now. I'm relieved but also exhausted from the tense anticipation and my self-imposed rehearsal, which continues to reverberate in my head with a muddle of German words. I still watch the squiggly, white-gloved finger pointing now to the right, now to the left. To the left, I see boys either younger than I or frailer, trying to sway his fateful decision as they plead with him in thin voices and in fractured German that they were gainfully employed in various ghetto productions. But he is deaf to their protests and pleadings. In vain, they keep stretching their scrawny arms to show that they are strong enough for hard work. They must scuttle over instantly to their newly assigned column or suffer brutal blows from the assisting SS men. Those who may try to protest or beseech the implacable officer will probably give up this idea just to avoid getting seriously hurt, because those who didn't, now stand in agony, moaning and holding their bruised or bleeding body parts.

Our column is now being marched off from the depot. I catch sight of a sign on an arched entrance, *Arbeit Macht Frei,* whose message that *Work Will Set You Free* reassures me that as long as we work, we'll be free of care – a slogan so well describing the proverbial German industriousness and purposefulness. There's a contradiction in it because you are not free when you are tied to your work; yet, at the same time, when you are totally absorbed in your work, you are free from all other concerns. So be it!

We'll see what work that will be.

Chapter 4:
Cesiek

As we leave the platform in an orderly column of five men abreast, I notice that one SS man guarding our flanks looks vaguely familiar. His narrow eyes and slim pug-nose set on a fleshy face and beefy neck remind me of Cesiek, the concierge's son from 63 Wolczanska Street, my yard playmate – the one who used to fetch me to play as he was taking, with great gusto, huge bites of a raw onion he held in one hand and a slab of bread he held in the other. I haven't seen him in five years since we were isolated from the Poles. It's hard to tell how he has changed in these formative years. But as a Pole, Cesiek couldn't be an SS man. Well, maybe. His last name, Szajder, signified German ancestry and would spell Scheider in German. Maybe he or his dad claimed to stem from a German stock to earn their status as *Volksdeutsche* (ethnic Germans living outside Germany), which would entitle them to all the privileges granted to native Germans, even serving in the SS.

Cesiek here?! Maybe if he saw me, he could do something for me. But he wouldn't recognize me all changed from a well-fed twelve-year-old to an emaciated scarecrow of seventeen. I'd have to tell him first who I am. But what if it isn't Cesiek? His face is typical of many Germans and Poles. He'll clobber me for just staring at him, let alone addressing him as "Cesiek". I check myself from calling out his name. What if he spurns me like my childhood playmate, Klaus Kinski did in the park after he became a Hitler Youth? What if he has to prove to his comrades that, as a true Nazi and a hardened SS man, he isn't bound by any regards for a former playmate, especially a Jewish one? He may not even want to admit that he ever associated with Jews. And to prove himself a worthy SS trooper, he may even act excessively harsh with me. He may even gloat that I, the spoiled, orange-fed momma's boy from a spacious apartment have met my well-deserved fate, while he, the janitor's son from a crammed cellar flat, fed on dry bread and onions, is now in the ranks of the most privileged, eating to his fullest and able to dispense brutality at will.

"*Los! Schnell! Auftreten! Los!* (Move! Faster! Step up! Move!)" An SS man's rifle butt pokes the back of the man in front of me. I quicken my trot to evade blows and stop staring at "Cesiek" who may find my gaze offensive and whack me. Even if it's him, he may see the reversal of our fortunes as an act of divine justice: by a magic stroke of Hitler's racial wand, Cesiek, a Pole, became an ethnic German, a regular blue-blood, a true scion of Aryan-Germanic ancestry, while Jews were relegated to being a scourge and a pestilence. Cesiek's janitor father must have been pleased to quit his job of sweeping the yard and stairs, rising at night to open the gate for latecomers, and cleaning public toilets. He could now join the "Master Race" and "put the Jews in their place" as Hitler had claimed he'd do if given the power to run the world.

"*Schnell! Schnell! Auftreten! Los!*" The rifle pokes the back of a man next to me.

But I may be wrong, maybe even envious that Poles of possible German ancestry were given a choice, while we Jews never had one. For all I know, Cesiek's dad may still be cleaning public toilets. Only now he is free of Jews; only Aryan tenants dwell in Lodz. Who knows what became of Cesiek and his caretaker parents?

"*Los! Los! Schneller! Schneller!*" We're prodded toward the camp urgently and more brutally as we're passing some smoldering pits, which emanate a sickening stench. A most horrid exhalation! What is this revolting smell? Is it some chemically treated garbage? It's hard to see what's in them because of all the smoke and vapors hanging densely over them. And the SS men are furiously speeding up our march to a fast trot while hitting us with the butts of their rifles and shouting at the top of their hoarse voices: "*Los! Los! Schneller machen! Los, los, ihr Sauhunde!* (Move! Move! Faster! Move, you scum!)".

Nah, I'm probably mistaken about Cesiek. I'm just too eager to find a friendly soul anywhere, even an SS man. Suddenly I feel terribly lonely without Mama and our extended family, even lonelier among all these strange men. Bereft of their closest and dearest ones, they surely feel like I do and are thinking of their mothers, daughters and other fragile female relatives now in the hands of these bestial thugs.

Chapter 5:
Where's Rozenblat

We finally reach a vast field in front of some massive barracks. Now, standing in long rows, we face a row of women who also just passed the selection successfully. An area about the width of a soccer field separates us from each other. Some tall, burly men in prison stripes, who are obviously in charge here, walk among us urging in Yiddish to hand over our valuables, hard currency, gold and jewelry. They alternately cajole and threaten, promising special privileges to those who'll voluntarily submit their valuables, and dreadful consequences to those who won't. Are they serious? Who'd still have any valuables left after five long years in the ghetto where we would've gladly swapped our last gem for a scarce piece of bread? But they keep urging, pleading, threatening.

One of them, a beefy hulk of a man, combs our ranks, searching for someone, coming up close to each of us and quizzing us intently in a crude Yiddish growl: "Where's Rozenblat, your Chief of Police? Where's that son of a whore? I was told that he came on this transport!" He disappears suddenly, but soon emerges again, urging: "Which one of you knows where Commandant Rozenblat is? Let me just find him and lay my hands on him. He put me away years ago, that son of a whore. Me, he put away. Me, Moishe Husyd. Because of him I'm here. Where is he, where?"

His voice turns ominous as he snarls: "Our woes should only last so long as he'll last in here, once I find him. I've been waiting here for his arrival all this time. Where's that son of a whore?" He scrutinizes each of us, searchingly, almost imploringly, but I'm not even sure how the Chief looks. He was probably second to Rumkowski in wielding power in the ghetto and must have arrived in the same car with the King. I wouldn't recognize him because he wasn't as notorious as King Chaim in the ghetto.

He disappears again, searching on. One of the men, with whom I just arrived, remarks to another: "I heard of him. That's Moishe Husyd. He used to be a well-known pimp in Lodz before the war."

So here's an ex-pimp, expelled from the ghetto as a convicted criminal some years ago, who has managed to make somewhat of a career for himself in here. He's hefty, so hunger is not a problem for him. He is fit and in good health, moving with remarkable agility for a man of his bulk. There's a feral flexibility about him, that of a panther on the prowl. And most of all, he seems to be quite at ease with the SS officers who are always hovering nearby. He's flitting freely from our side to the women's column across the field – one may wonder what for? He's not going to find Chief Rozenblat in there! Maybe he still plies his pre-war trade here, too, supplying the SS with sexual consorts? If he's in charge here then surely the SS aren't averse in utilizing the professional skills of their captive Jews, no matter how base they are – even pimps and felons.

Chapter 6:
I'm with the Young

As my eyes follow Moishe walking sprightly to the women now, I notice Mama, standing with her bundle in a long row of women facing us. Our eyes lock. Apparently, she has been watching me, always concerned about my safety and well-being.

"Mietek! I'm with the young!" she exclaims jubilantly, glad that I finally spotted her. She seems much relieved at her fortunate selection as if it has given her a guarantee to survive the war. With her triumphant exclamation, she encourages me that she's still around and that we may reunite some day. I'm not surprised. I never expected Mama, with her good looks, still pert and energetic, to be assigned anywhere but "with the young". It never occurred to me that she may be taken away or die, just as it has been unthinkable for me to envision my own death. Yet her reassuring words dismay me, for I sense the pain of those who heard her but from whom, just a short time ago, their own loved ones were torn away either because they were too young, too old or too frail. I now fear that proverbial evil-eye because she dared to voice her joy in a place such as this.

I send Mama a quick nod and a glimpse of acknowledgement, then quickly lower my eyes lest I attract some envious glances from those near me whose mothers didn't qualify to remain "with the young". I don't want them to know that I am that lucky youngster to whom this mother shouted her good fortune. To avert their envy, I don't even return her jubilant cry that I, too, am "with the young and the fit". In a place such as this, any display of joy is an affront to all around. I'm taking another farewell glimpse of her so that I'll retain her cherished image forever, just in case… Oh, God, please let Mama's lucky selection not only keep her among the young and the able-bodied, but also among the living. until we meet again.

Could these be Mama's last words to me? Will I ever see her again? Are these few encouraging words "I'm with the young!" to be her legacy? Is staying young and fit the great secret to survival? She has just assured me that she'll go on living and that I mustn't worry, that she'll be watching over me again, restoring my faith in an orderly universe where mothers and children stay together forever.

But she must be distraught that they took me away from her – her sole purpose in life. Now that she's cut off from all her sisters, brothers, their children, and left a widow and fatherless, I realize that I am the only one who has any meaning for her. And from the way she doted on me, pampered and indulged me all these years, I think that she'll be inconsolable without me. A feeling of guilt comes over me for having wanted recently to become independent of her. But I rationalize that I wished it for her own sake so that she wouldn't have to share her own food rations with me anymore – as she always did.

I'm about to look up and send her another reassuring glance that I'm okay and that she shouldn't worry, that I'll be careful – her frequent admonition to me – when an unusual sight attracts my attention…

Chapter 7:
The Hopping Chief

"**H**op, hop, hop like a frog, you son of a whore!"

We all turn our eyes in the direction of this booming command in Yiddish and witness a grotesque spectacle. In the center of the field, between us and the women, a man is squatting. He's stark naked except for a ghetto policeman's hat on his head. With both hands, he clenches, like a scepter, an ordinary straw broom with its bristles up. Towering over him is the stocky Moishe Husyd, bellowing commands. A few striped henchmen stand on the side, enjoying the sight with sadistic glee. The man is forced to take giant frog leaps with the broom in his hands.

"Hop! Hop like a frog, you son of a whore! Hop! Hop! Just like that!" Moishe Husyd is delighted with his own ingenuity. "And with each jump, shout loud and clear in German: I'm Rozenblat, Commander-in-Chief of the Litzmannstadt Ghetto Police! Come on, now, shout, you dignified son of a whore! Loud! Louder!!!"

We now recognize that the naked, leaping man in the blue and yellow striped hat, bearing the insignia of our Ghetto Chief of Police and clasping a broom with both hands, is indeed Leon Rozenblat, for whom Moishe Husyd was searching just moments ago. The sight is unbearably humiliating for the chief, especially before all the women who surely must be shocked by his nakedness. But the hefty Husyd and his fellow henchmen, as well as some amused SS men, are all having a great time. I'm shocked to see the chief who, with that broom, looks pathetic in his naked disgrace. With each leap, his policeman's hat totters on his head while his scrotum grotesquely flaps forwards and backwards like a clapper of a frantically tolling bell, rising up with each forward flap and hitting against his buttocks on each return. It's a demeaning display in front of all our dazed new arrivals. And Moishe eagerly scans our faces for an approval of his ingenuous side-show. He seems to encourage us to join him in his revelry. "Jump! Jump, you son of a whore!" he roars, his voice booming over the huge field, as we look on embarrassed and incredulous for the hapless chief. "Shout louder! Louder!!" he bellows, though the chief is already hoarse from the strain.

"I am Rozenblat, the Commander-in-Chief of the Litzmannstadt Ghetto Police," he obediently shouts in German, magnifying the absurdity of his position. The Chief keeps frog-hopping between our two rows that stretch through the length of a soccer field, uttering these ridiculous words over and over. Moishe, who is in complete control of this repugnant exhibition and of his goons, must be totally gratified with his vengeance by now. If a felon has ever gotten even with the one responsible for his banishment and imprisonment, surely this creepy circus can prove it.

I try looking for Mama to see how this dreadful scene has affected her, but she's no longer to be seen in the long row of women across. She was probably moved to the next stage of our processing. I wonder if I will ever see her again, but quickly drop this thought because the alternative is unbearable to consider. She must be thinking the same right now. My absence must be devastating for her. I must hold on to her photos, or her cherished image may blur in my memory forever.

Chapter 8:
The Processing

The "zebras" prod us on into a nearby barrack, and we leave this lurid spectacle. In the anteroom, they inform us that we are in the shower barrack and must disrobe and leave all our belongings and clothes on the floor, right where we stand, keeping nothing but our belts and shoes. Again they urge us to hand over any valuables that we may still have on us. Some men hand over their wedding bands. I suddenly realize that my knapsack with the diary I kept in the ghetto, my treasured stamp collection, and my favorite family pictures may be lost forever. I must save the photos to preserve the memories just in case we'll never see each other again. I must preserve the past if only to reminisce that I too once had a life. I reach into my knapsack on the floor and pull out a handful of photos, select a few most precious ones, and put them into my shoe.

"Aha! Gotcha, you son-of-a-bitch!" A smashing whack to the side of my head. I reel to the left, but regain balance before falling. There's a ringing in my right ear. "Hand over that shoe!" bellows a husky zebra orderly. In all this commotion, his watchful eyes didn't miss my concealment. He turns my shoe over and shakes its contents onto his hand. The photos drop out onto his hand and spill onto the floor. He tosses them down from his palm without even looking at them and disappears among the disrobing men as suddenly as he came. I think of picking up the scattered photos, but dread getting whacked again by him or some other alert orderly among us watching our every move. In a rush to disrobe, other men drop their clothing on my strewn pictures, so I'd have trouble retrieving them anyway. Surely, my photos will be destroyed here as just that much trash; one's most cherished mementoes are another's refuse.

All these lovely, dear faces to admire when I'd look for comfort in my unexpected loneliness. I feel as if I and my whole past too are being buried with all these precious pictures under a smelly pile of men's clothing.

"You little son-of-a-bitch, you're holding out on us?!" roars a husky zebra at a boy, distracting my thoughts. "I was told that you arrived here with a load of valuables."

"It's not true. I don't have any valuables." He turns his coat and pants pockets inside out. His boyish voice turns plaintive: "Here! You can see for yourself."

He looks like Michal Rusek, the younger brother of Maniek Rusek, who was a top-notch soccer player and ping-pong ace, whose style I used to admire in the early years of the ghetto in the sports club on Lutomierska Street.

"Open up your whorish snout!" the collector orders and Michal complies. "Aha! What's that?! Gimme that gold tooth. Come on! On the double!"

"How can I give you my tooth? Here look, I'm trying but it won't move, see?"

The zebra's fist crashes into the lad's cheek with a crunch. Blood sputters and the boy spits out some teeth on the palm of his hand. "See how simple and easy it is, you son of a whore? Now gimme that tooth!" And without waiting for the boy's reaction, he picks up the bloody gold tooth from Michal's gory palm and saunters away. Tears well up on the boy's bloodied face.

We are rushed into the next room. Some men, still trying to retrieve items from their clothing left in heaps on the floor, are being mercilessly flogged and ordered to leave everything behind. I'm probably lucky for leaving my family photos on the floor, or else I, too, would get a beating. We proceed to the next room, which looks like an anteroom to showers with steam coming out and the sound of splashing water. But before going there, we must undergo a thorough bodily shaving.

Here, prisoner-barbers stand with the tools of their trade, clipping off all our hair. We stand naked in line before them, waiting our turn to sit down on little taborets, which look like the ones I helped to mass produce in the Ghetto Tischlerei (Ghetto Joiner's Workshop) two years ago. We are shorn, then they shave our heads, chins, under arms and pubic regions. The barbers work swiftly with blunted razors and without lathering the areas to be shaved; they just wet a soft brush in a soapy solution and often shave too close, leaving our men with bleeding patches of lacerated skin. I'm lucky; in spite of my seventeen years, I still don't have any facial, pubic, or underarm hair. Perhaps the lack of proper nourishment in the last five years has stunted my normal body development. Meanwhile, the processed men moan and groan as they bleed from their scalps, faces and scrotums.

After the shaving, we line up to have all our shaven places disinfected, which the orderlies do with brushes dipped in buckets with some smelly, caustic solution, then smear it into our groins, armpits, faces and heads. My shaven head must have been also lacerated because it's stinging in places from this caustic disinfectant.

Next we must pass an inspection for hidden valuables in the most private areas of our body. Another zebra, specialized in body search, checks our mouths under tongues; then another expert orders us to turn around and spread the cheeks of our buttocks. The concept of inserting valuables into one's rectum is unknown to me. But people are obviously quite resourceful. And at first, I thought that this was just a medical check-up.

The women, too, surely must endure this abject procedure, and if I find it offensive, how degraded the young girls must feel to bare their privates to these callous brutes! It may be just my wishful thinking that there are women searchers and barbers because there were no women zebras in charge when we stood outside. Only Moishe Husyd rambled freely from the men's rows to the women's, so the men must be in charge there, too. Ghastly!

They prompt us into another anteroom, which is part bathroom. We proceed as if in a chaotic trance. There's no chaos here, but a definite order in the systematic progression of our processing. It's the sudden impact of family loss and the violation of our privacy by these felonious brutes that creates the sense of utter disorientation in us.

We now enter the showers in groups of about fifty. "Wash up! Wash up!" shout the zebras in charge. "Now you may be needed for labor, so your chances of living longer are better." They say it matter-of-factly and without sarcasm.

Chapter 9:
The Chief Tortured

At once, Moishe Husyd and three burly henchmen barge into the anteroom prodding the naked chief with the scepter-broom. They stop and gather right before me and my group. I can now see the chief closely; he looks about fifty and fit with a sinewy, well-proportioned body that bears no signs of malnutrition like ours. Moishe bellows in Yiddish: "*Fetch Janek Tsygan!*" and one of his three cohorts exits and promptly returns with another huge, robust, swarthy zebra, which probably earned him his nickname, tsygan, or gypsy, in Polish. He's equal to Husyd in bulk and, like him, exudes agility and great physical strength. His rugged good looks, self-assurance and precise, deliberate movements indicate that he, like Moishe, has authority here.

With a powerful blow of his fist to Rozenblat's temple, the hefty Husyd lays him out on the stony floor. The dull thud of the collapse brings an instant hush to the room. "Our woes should last only so long as this whore's son has still left to live," Husyd intones, looking up as if in a prayer, then snatches a belt from one of the new arrivals standing near me; he tosses it to one of his squat henchmen who tucks the chief's ankles into it and lifts his lower body off the floor. Another henchman lifts Rozenblat by the head with both hands. Both begin swinging the naked chief as if they were about to toss him into a swimming pool, while Husyd and Tsygan, who flank him on both sides, keep delivering powerful fist blows to his sides. Rozenblat's battered torso swings like a hammock. At Husyd's behest, they now switch places; with Tsygan swinging the chief by the head, Husyd by the belt over the ankles, and the two cohorts deliver jabs to Rozenblat's flanks.

"Let the poor chief go already!" Moishe says to Janek with mock pity. Tsygan raises Rozenblat's head up high, then lets it drop. The head crashes to the concrete floor while Moishe is still holding up the ankles. Moishe grins broadly, delighted with his ambiguous command. The other three torturers are also amused at Rozenblat's torment. Moishe gets the broomstick with which Rozenblat had to leap-frog outside and lays it across the prostrate chief's neck. He then steps on it, balancing his hefty body, and rocking slowly and deliberately over Rozenblat's throat as if trying to sever it from the rest of the body. The chief's face turns blue. His body begins twitching. The hefty Husyd adroitly jumps off the ends of the broomstick and scrutinizes his now motionless victim. But Rozenblat's chest starts heaving and a gurgle-like sound emerges from his throat. A flicker of life surprisingly returns to him. Moishe lifts the torso by its head and motions to Janek to raise it by its feet. After hoisting it up to his chin, Moishe lets it drop again. There's a resounding crack as the skull hits the concrete, and Rozenblat's face instantly turns a deep blue, then ashen. Another gurgling noise comes out of his throat. There are a few more twitches that soon stop as life is now seemingly fast leaving Rozenblat's battered body. Moishe puts his foot directly on Rozenblat's throat, pressing it down; then jumps on his chest, bouncing on it with all of his massive bulk. He tramples the throat again, twisting and crumpling his foot as if to squash a bug or extinguish a cigarette. But the chief shows no signs of life anymore, and Moishe quickly steps off.

"Oh, no, you don't!" he roars in Yiddish. "You aren't going to die just yet!" Carefully he watches for a sign of life. In his paroxysm of sadistic abandon, Moishe nevertheless seems enough in control of himself to ease up when life is about to expire and deprive him of his torturing act. He seems to know exactly when to stop the ferocious torment. His expertise indicates that he must have done it many times before. Surely enough, a rush of air fills his victim's lungs, the chest begins to heave, and a gurgle comes out of his throat, cresting his blue lips with a pink froth. It's as if he wants his victim to die a hundred times. He jumps on Rozenblat's rib cage as if trying to cave it in under his heft. He jumps again and again. It's amazing how he keeps up his balance. The chief may be dead at last because his battered body is still. But only Moishe knows for sure. He ties the belt around the chief's bluish neck and starts to drag him away as we stand incredulous and stupefied at this spectacle of wanton murder.

"*Achtung!*" A thunderous command to attention whips us at once with its urgency. It's shouted by two zebras near the door who are already at attention in military fashion. Now we, civilian prisoners, too, must act like soldiers to conform with the Germans' love of militarism. Reacting instantly to the electrifying *"Achtung!"* we draw ourselves up, tense our naked bodies, push out our chests and chins and suck in our dried up bellies. A hush falls over the bathhouse. We look straight ahead, yet see a fairly young and lean SS officer striding in jauntily, as if propelled on springs. He exudes self-assurance and authority. His face beams in a bemused expression, as if watching circus clowns, yet his eyes are cold, remorseless and alert enough to let nothing escape his attention. Without slackening his snappy stride, he scans the goings-on, seemingly bored by its routine and obvious familiarity. As he briskly walks by us, Moishe, still grasping the belt around Rozenblat's neck and brimming with cheerfulness, shouts out in military fashion – but with mock gravity and fake regret – *"Ich melde gehorchsam dass der Herr Kommandant der Ghetto Polizei hat sich eben aufgehongen.* (I'm dutifully reporting that the Chief of the Ghetto Police has just hung himself)."

Without slowing his brisk gait or changing his bemused expression, the SS officer mutters something to Moishe, which I'm close enough to catch as *"Mach mal zu!* (Get it over with!)" But his command lacks a sense of real urgency as he's obviously amused by Moishe's mocking tone and his facetious report of Rozenblat's suicide. It's clear that he's well aware of the bestial display that has just taken place, but acknowledges Moishe's joke as a clever way with which a court jester would report and entertain his lord and master.

With Moishe dragging the body by the belt around its neck, they all disappear from view. I'm stunned by what I've just seen. Things have been happening so quickly that I don't even have time to reflect upon them. Here, right before me, a foul murder has just been committed. A man has been brutally tortured to death. A human life has been taken right here. I'd never witnessed an act of torture in my life, not even in the five years of ghetto shootings and hangings, and yet I watched it now with hardly a sign of emotion. But maybe it's better this way. Any display of excitement, sympathy, pity or even grief in these strange surroundings may expose me as a weakling not fit to live among real men.

Chapter 10:
Rice and Milk

We are now in the shower room. The water is scalding, and I dart away from under it. As if in a trance, my hands begin washing my wet body without any soap. From another room, Moishe's voice bellows to us in Yiddish through the noise of splashing water: "And your Rumkowski crapped in his pants from fear before I laid him out, too."

Thus ends our hope that nothing bad would befall a transport with our King on it. He was our only hope that the Nazis weren't deceiving us when we volunteered for the final train out of the ghetto. And now. Rumkowski is *dead*! But if Moishe wants us to rejoice at his end as that of a collaborationist, I feel only sadness as all hope is lost now. I didn't think he'd be killed. But, like the rest of us, I thought he'd do some sort of productive labor or even still be in charge of us. To hear him slain after five years of servility to his German masters, and at the hands of Moishe Husyd, a petty criminal..., a fellow Jew...!?

For five long years, Rumek tried to save us from total destruction; bargaining with the Nazis when they demanded large transports of deportees; trying to spare the community as a whole by complying with orders to weed out the sick, the old, the very young and others whom the Nazis regarded unfit for labor. And his reward? Befouling himself from terror before a Jewish felon of the Lodz underworld, who can now kill with impunity and who surely regards his slaughter of Rozenblat and Rumkowski as justified vengeance. Maybe once he, too, shook with fear before the likes of Police Chief Rozenblat and Rumkowski, but now the King not only shook before him but even "crapped" from fear...a great triumph for Moishe the Pimp! Soiling oneself – a human's ultimate disgrace, which assures the tormentor that he wields supreme power and terror. Nothing could have pleased Moishe more before he finished off the dethroned "King". And now brags about it, passing himself off as our avenger.

Suddenly, a beefy, hairy arm thrusts a big red bowl into my hands. The metal dish contains steaming rice and...and...can it be milk!? I haven't seen milk in five years since the closing of the ghetto in the beginning of 1940. The rice is so dense that the tin tablespoon in it is standing upright. Can this be a dream? Am I raving? My eyes are still dazed from witnessing the brutal murder. Yet, here's a steaming bowl, rice and milk. All so inviting. Just dip the spoon into the rice and raise it to my mouth. Once it lands in my cavernous stomach, I shall know whether it's a dream or not. My eyes follow the beefy outstretched arm to its owner.

No! It can't be!! The man offering me this heavenly feast is none other than – Moishe Husyd! "Here, eat!" he says matter-of-factly in Yiddish, as if he's been handing it to me for years. I dare not refuse him, nor do I intend to. But I seem hesitant, for he again pushes the blessed bowl right at my chest, repeating encouragingly: "Gobble it up!"

As if in a trance, I accept it with both hands, nodding thankfully; I put a spoonful of steaming rice and milk into my mouth, marveling at the divine taste. If anything makes sense here, it's the blissful feeling of an appeased stomach. So real, so very real. Manna from heaven! My innards greedily welcome this unreal feast, though I enjoy it less as I notice that the naked men crowding me respectfully move away to give me more room, surely wondering why only I was singled out for such a treat. But I just keep gobbling it up. Later I may try to figure out, "Why me." Voraciously, greedily, with immense gulps, I wolf down spoonfuls of this delicious concoction, lest it be taken from me. Warm milk! Thick with rice! Ah! The taste of milk.

Chapter 11:
In Stripes

We are led forward to a storeroom where they give us camp outfits: a cap, a jacket and pants, all in blue and white stripes, all used, and some quite worn out. But they let us keep our shoes and the belt. No underwear or socks. The functionaries in there have a weird sense of humor; they dole out oversize garments to small men and undersize ones to taller men. But our new arrivals quickly swap them with each other. Not all are lucky enough, however, to find suitable swappers, and those who don't, look ridiculous and pathetic. Men who arrived in shiny black riding boots – a status symbol in the ghetto worn by factory directors, high administration officials and the prosperous Special Police – must turn them in for clogs without laces.

We are chased outside and put in formation. Darkness has fallen. A faint distant light is visible from lamps up high. We march toward the camp, but more actually are driven like cattle by the SS guards. Those with their just-gotten clogs, clomp and hobble, barely keeping up with the brisk tempo. Their clippety-clop gets the attention of abusive SS men who prod and hit them with rifle butts. This trips them up, as their un-laced clogs slide off, slowing their pace, which goads the guards to beat and kick them some more.

I'm lucky to wear a good pair of used shoes that Uncle Ignatz gave me just before deportation. He donned a brand new pair of shiny black riding boots himself, made either for this trip or even long before, but never had worn them, I am sure, because they were so daunting to ordinary ghetto people. They signified power and cost a lot. To think that Uncle Ignatz could still afford to make such a purchase after all these years of starvation! Maybe the four Lawits, cooped up in their narrow little kitchen next to our room, didn't suffer such hunger as Mama and I did – and Dad, who starved to death three years ago.

Mama got my old shoes in a swap with somebody, but was swindled. Surely she had to swap some of her bread rations for them. They looked good, but soon fell apart and were no better than my previous ones, which I always had to stuff with wads of paper to cover the gaping holes. Yet I was still better off than many others who wrapped their feet in rags, barely dragging their bulky weight on their swollen limbs. But my uncle's used shoes are solid, and I'm able to keep up with the trot and evade the whacks of the prodding SS.

My stripes fit me right. I tied the loose pants with my belt and now am running along briskly. How simple it is to fit into another outfit. As I grew bigger in the last five years, I got no new clothes but wore Dad's. In the blissful pre-war days, it took several fittings at the fashionable Migdal Tailors before Mama decided that my suit was made just right.

The sky is dark. It's pitch black save for sparks and flames spewing from tall smokestacks. The air is heavy with strange vapors and a sickly stench that envelopes everything. It reminds me of an odor from before the war when housewives singed the feathers of a slaughtered fowls' skin.

The frequent shrieks and moans from our rushed men indicate that the SS rifle butts are in constant motion. An image of devils in hell prodding sinners with tridents flashes through my mind. Behind us, from somewhere maybe near the smokestacks, I hear a muffled, mournful, torturous wail from a thousand women. Or do I? Whether it is real or not, I know that I'll remember this moment if I live for an eternity. I ardently beseech God to spare Mama.

Chapter 12:
On the Barrack Floor

Our trot ends in front of one of many barracks and we are chased into its cavernous bowels. It has no furnishings on its barren concrete floor or even windows, but instead there is a row of skylights. A tiny room in a corner has a couple of blanketed bunk-beds for functionaries. A dim light bulb near the high ceiling stresses the barrack's eerie desolation.

"*Hinlegen! Hinlegen! Hinlegen!* (Lie down! Lie down! Lie down!)" The German command to lie down is instantly followed by cracks of clubs on human bones before we realize that the SS guards are gone and that our new tormentors in zebra stripes are inmates just like us. We're terrified and immediately drop to the concrete floor to evade their merciless blows. At once, the floor fills up with wall-to-wall bodies. Those who hesitate to drop down on top of the others get singled out for an extra cascade of crushing blows with cudgels and bats. The orderlies in this barrack have an amazing ability to step over a vortex of human bodies without even tripping. They pounce on anyone still on his feet. We stay on top of others, creating a billowing whirl of bodies. The orderlies relish the muddle of stumbling human figures as if they were little kids thrilled by watching falling dominoes.

One orderly, towering over us, watches intently for those still up. As soon as someone rises to only a half-sitting position, he delivers devastating blows with his cudgel. He's well nourished and emanates strength and physical fitness. His round face, beefy neck and huge arms, now elongated with that ubiquitous club, look ominous to a bunch of emaciated scarecrows like us. He seems to have no scruples about abusing us and, with total abandon, lashes out in violent outbursts. I search his face for an expression of some humanity. After all, he, too, is only a prisoner. But all I see is an ordinary face, smug and determined, seeking thrills while emulating his SS masters in wielding power over us.

There are hundreds of us wedged so tightly that we overlap on others just as in the cattle-car last night. Again we're crouching and crushing each other's limbs. Those bleeding from wounds inflicted by the SS rifle butts plead for water, but are told that the washroom-barrack is shut till morning. When the hubbub dies down at last, the inmate/orderlies introduce themselves as Kameraden Polizei (Comrade Police), or kapos for short, and the caveman as Block-Aelteste, or Barrack Boss, who wields total control of everybody in it.

We spend the night in pain, magnified by worry about our female or male relatives who were taken from us during the selection. But at least my stomach is full on Moishe Husyd's rice with milk. No one got any food since we were chased out of the train at dawn and, now that we are here for the night, no one will receive any till morning. I think of Mama's long fast and her concern for me. If she only knew that I had such a royal feast in the bathhouse, she'd allay her worries and endure better.

How does Husyd have access to such food? Did the SS order him to kill Rumek? Did they put him in charge because they knew that he was a brutal killer? How did they know? If Hitler is so keen on law and order, why do they tolerate felons, and Jewish ones at that? Do they purposely give the Jewish underworld a free hand here to prey on their own kind to eventually destroy itself? And why did Husyd single me out for this treat? To clear his conscience by an act of charity? Maybe that's why they call him "Husyd" – or the pious one? Maybe he just felt sorry for me as I stood there innocently staring at how he snuffed out a human life?

Why don't they put in charge industrious administrators such as King Rumek, who turned a virtual waste of broken-down workshops and equipment into the most efficient and most economic mass-producing Jewish entity?

Chapter 13:
The Eager Henchmen

I'm dead tired and want to sleep, but the concrete floor is cold, hard and I can't shake free of elbows, knees and feet that are pinning me down. I'm trapped like an insect in a spider's web. The moans and groans magnify this ghastly nightmare. All these strangers intensify my loneliness. It is another night without sleep.

"*Aufstehen! Aufstehen!* (Rise up! Rise up!)" But it seems like we just lay down a couple of hours ago! The muffled calls come from the kapos' room and are almost solicitous, as if they mean to let us indulge in some more rest. Yet, in an instant, they're followed by a cannonade of thuds: Crack! Bang! Bam! The kapos erupt from their lair and sow mayhem, swinging clubs right and left. As if air-borne, without slipping or falling, they hop on our billowing, bony bodies and deliver crushing blows with their thrashing cudgels. These bat-swinging devils are in a frenzy of bone cracking. Bang! Bam! Thump the clubs against human bodies – a lashing orgy of sadism and brute force. How can they be so deft at stomping chests, arms, legs and bellies without tripping up? Their agility seems supernatural. Terrorized, we spring to our feet pushing, jostling, kicking and scrambling over each other to get away from the kapos with their mayhem-sowing clubs. Stiff from cramped positions, we can't get up fast enough. Luckily, I'm lying far from their little room and by the time they reach me, I'm up and standing. Their calls to rise were muffled so that they could sneak up on us and thresh us before we had a chance to stand up. It's an eerie wake-up call in the middle of an eerie night. The subdued rousing calls, the thuds of clubs, and the shrieks of pain are the sounds heralding our new day.

We're chased outside into a dark night. It must still be hours before sunrise. With nothing to do, we huddle to avoid the wind and the chill. Everyone tries to squeeze inside the circle to be shielded by another's body. Why did they rush us out so early if there's nothing to do? Stars are still studding the inky sky and the sparks from the tall stacks are soaring toward them. Our herd expands with more men, which are now shielding me from the chill. Without shirts, underwear and socks, we shiver in this brisk air and cling closer to each other, joking that we're a bunch of grapes.

It doesn't look like we're going anywhere. The early wake-up call was apparently just to deprive us of a full night's rest even though it was impossible to sleep in the crammed barrack anyway. We spend hours standing in this huddle as the sky lightens. Now we can see one another. Like grotesque masks some blood-smeared faces appear among us – the result of last night's and this morning's clubbings. Standing compressed amid groaning, ghoulish-looking and drowsing men in this early dawn is nightmarish.

As the morning brightens, we see contours of mountains. Maybe that's why the air is so chilly. Around us I see an infinity of barracks just like ours. In front of each stand, just as we do, thousands of men. Some sections of barracks are isolated by electrical barbed-wire fences; a true city of barracks with thousands of inmates. Perched above on four stilts are guard towers. The air is fouled by a sickly stench flowing non-stop from a black river of billowing smoke, laced occasionally with flames from the tall stacks. Even though the smoke rises, the fetid odor hangs low, filling our nostrils and lungs.

At last, the kapos tell us to assemble for the morning *Appell* (assembly); later there's also to be an evening assembly. They arrange us in formations, and we stand at attention awaiting the count, while the kapos perform their grisly work of delivering furious beatings to anyone who steps out of his place in the ranks.

"*Muetzen ab*! (Caps off!)" In one singular clap, we slap our right thighs with caps in hand. We doff our caps to this command as a gesture of respect to the SS officer who walks up to receive the count. Later, we put them back on with the same loud hand slap on "*Muetzen auf*! (Caps on!)" If anyone's slap is a second off, he's taken out of line and given a thorough beating, after which he becomes even less likely to keep in sync. It seems that the SS men here have nothing better to do than play at pointless military drills with a bunch of exhausted and starved civilian inmates. Instead of putting us to productive work so that they can go into battle to defend their Fatherland, they are just killing time here – and us – to boot.

When the SS are riled by an inmate, they take his number – our new identification numbers, sewn on the left side of our jackets – for later punishment. We no longer have family or first names. Our self-esteem is erased with this last obliteration of our personal identity. Without our belongings, our hair, and clad in these ill-fitting stripes, we're beyond recognition. We feel insignificant and ludicrous. Yet we stand erect and all tensed up. All former distinctions of rank, social status, wealth and even age are gone. The SS officer receives count also of the battered bodies on the ground. The kapos seem proud of their mayhem. If this keeps up, there'll be much more room on the floor to sleep.

After Appell, we're given bowls and "breakfast"; no food, just a tepid liquid euphemistically called coffee. We're then ordered to the Lavatory Barrack in groups of fifty where we relieve ourselves and where the injured can at last wash their wounds. There's neither soap nor towels. In the middle of this huge barrack, runs a long wooden plank with round holes over a fetid ditch. The holes are so close that while sitting on one we touch the next man. The watchful kapos rush us and chase off lingerers, whacking them to speed up their bowel movement: "Others are waiting!" Some men are chased off even before they're done, which adds to their misery and humiliation. Too shy to defecate in public or on the kapo's command, I sit over the hole with my pants down, just to rest up a bit from all the standing in the morning. Even in the ghetto, the public outhouse had a door for privacy. I'm sitting next to a short man whose oversized jacket makes him look even smaller. He's Kaufman, the Ghetto Fire Chief, known as a brave fireman. Kaufman, just like the other larger-than-life ghetto bigwigs Rumkowski and Rozenblat, has suddenly shrunk to the size of an ordinary person. Before the death-disseminating SS in here, just as before the Grim Reaper, these former ghetto *prominents* are just so much offal to dispose of. Death doesn't choose favorites: One corpse is as good as another, one Jew just as another. But Kaufman sits seemingly unperturbed by the kapo's rushing. Can it be that his heroic and selfless stature in the ghetto works for him here, too? Sitting on a toilet undisturbed must clearly be a mark of distinction and privilege in here.

Chapter 14:
The Welcoming Committee

We, the new arrivals are starved. The "breakfast" was a sadistic pretention. We're sent to another barrack for orientation given by some kapos who snidely refer to themselves as the "Welcoming Committee". The first one explains the hierarchy of prisoner-functionaries and explains the various colors of the triangles sewn on our jackets: black for the asocial elements, purple for religious dissenters, pink for homosexuals, green for professional criminals, red for political prisoners. Ours are yellow to mark us as Jews and red to show that we're also political. So now, suddenly, we've advanced to "political" status. Never mind the Jewish career criminals, pederasts or converts to Christianity. If one is a Jew, he is "political". The kapo informs us that we will soon be selected for work in our skills and training, and sent away from this transit camp of Birkenau, a sub-camp of Auschwitz.

When he finishes, another kapo struts in. He beams as he scrutinizes us. But his cheerfulness is deceiving. He's not as nice and informative as the first kapo but a brutish, beefy thug, with a bullwhip, which he keeps slamming with a resounding whack into his massive hand. He, then, glares at each and every one of us. "How long do you think you'll last in here, eh?" He addresses us in German, and his green triangle shows him as a professional German criminal. No one volunteers an answer and he continues: "Three weeks at the most!" He pauses and glares to see if his morbid prediction has had an effect on us. "And you probably thought you were coming to a spa in the mountains, didn't you? Didn't you?!" he thunders, breaking the oppressive silence. "You're still very lucky," he goes on. "If you came here when I did some years ago, you wouldn't have lasted two days. *Two days*!!" he roars. "So you can bless your good fortune!"

"Where are our women and children?" shout our new arrivals, encouraged by the kapo's softer tone and his reminiscing.

"Up on their way to heaven!" he snaps back. "And if you think you can get out of here, there's only one way," and he points his whip upward. "Right through the chimney." He looks at us intently, slowly scanning every face for the effect of his words. They are met with silence. He raises his whip. "Who can tell me what is this thing that I have in my hand?"

Some men, encouraged by his sudden switch to a more chatty tone, eagerly respond:

"A riding crop!"

"A club!"

"A bullwhack!"

"A truncheon!"

"A knout!"

"A horsewhip!"

He's amused at the extent of clever guesses and pleased with himself that none is correct. He shakes his head in playful denial. The men, detecting his relenting demeanor and hoping to mellow him even further by playing his guessing game, venture with more synonyms. Eagerly, anxiously, like pupils in a classroom trying to please a pedantic teacher hoping, perhaps, to placate this beast in charge of our immediate fate, they shout,:

"A bat!"

"A quirt!"

"A mace!"

"A bullwhip!"

"A crop!"

The kapo keeps shaking his head. He relishes the chance to deny success to all those guessers with their clever synonyms. I'm impressed with their knowledge of German and even surprised that this language is so rich in synonyms for a simple whip.

"A cudgel!"

"A bludgeon!"

"A rod!"

"A flagellum!"

"A stave!"

"No!" he thunders after each answer. "*Das ist eine SCHLAG-MACHINE!* (This is a thrashing machine!)" he roars after a dramatic pause. And to stress its menacing meaning, he whacks the knout into his thick palm with a resounding crack. Pleased with himself for stumping us all, he glares at each and every one of us with a psychopath's intensity. As he neighs, gurgles and slobbers, his searching gaze seems to be asking: How did you like that bit of cleverness, eh? Not one of you robbed me of my punch line! All you clever guys with your knowledge of language! The moment is his; he's making the most of it. He showed us! He squeals with delight. What a creep!

"*Das ist eine Schlagmachine!*" he bellows again to underscore his victory and scans our faces, gloating over our failure to solve his riddle. He's so gross and so crass that I suspect he got this riddle from some clever SS man rather than coining it himself.

His upbeat mood abruptly shifts. He whacks the cudgel into his beefy palm and now scans us menacingly with a demented, predatory glare. It pleases him to see us flinch at that ominous crack, as his "thrashing machine" descends into his massive paw.

"Do you know where you are now?" he queries after strutting before us. No one answers him this time. Maybe he wants to stump us again. "In Auschwitz!" he thunders. "*Und hier wird ihr schon ausschwitzen* (And here you will duly sweat it out)," he declares with that triumphant look, again delighted with the cleverness of his pun in which he changed the name of the camp from a proper noun into a verb of sweating – *schwitzen* – and cracks the knout into his hand. This brute is a regular comedian. Only none of us is laughing. He alone is most pleased with his own drollery. "You saw the smoke. That's the only way that you'll ever get out of here." But he's repeating himself. Apparently fresh out of witticisms, he hands us over to the next one of his kapo cohorts for a proper "welcome".

This goon has none of his predecessor's gallows-humor and shifting of moods. He's simply abusive. Our presence here is a personal affront to this Jewish bully who addresses us in Yiddish for a change. "How dare you arrive here five minutes before twelve?" he hisses over and over as if this was a great secret. What is he hinting at? That we had a choice *not* to come?! He's pacing before us and repeating his question. All these questions! They seem like a test that we have to pass before gaining admittance to this exclusive camp "Five minutes before twelve," he reiterates, shaking his head in scornful disbelief. Obviously, he insinuates that we let the Hitlerites ship us here only in the last moments of war. But how were we to know it? Without radios, telephones or even newspapers, we couldn't rely on rumors. And just how could we have resisted, cut off from the rest of the world and hermetically sealed in the ghetto cage?

"You scum dare to show up here five minutes before twelve. You sons of whores come here at five to twelve!" he keeps harping on and on as if to imprint this sin of ours on our minds forever.

But what if we had known that the end was near? What if we had disobeyed the German orders for evacuation? Could we have hidden? Where? We couldn't have just crawled into some crevice and stayed there until the war was over. We'd have had to come out to get some food, most likely by begging from gentiles. There were rewards for reporting hidden Jews. And it would have been impossible for all the ghetto's remaining seventy thousand to hide. And resist? How? With what? Run out of the ghetto surrounded by sentries, posted every one hundred meters? And what about the women and children? How could they run? And even if we could have evaded the German bullets, who would have given us shelter?

Why is this brute nagging us with this pointless phrase? Before Germans we must bear our guilt for our racial sins and for whatever else they choose to blame us; before Christians for the death of Christ; and now we are guilty before our own fellow Jews for *coming here*!?

But the brute still isn't content with his rebuke. "Where do you think your parents are? They are on their way to heaven right now. Just look up when you are outside if you want to see them. And how long do you think you'll last here? No longer than two weeks. Tops, three."

No, that can't be. He surely intends to keep us in mental anguish just as the kapos in our home-barrack keep us in physical anguish. How can he talk to us like this? Where's his brotherly compassion for those of us who have just been torn away from our dearest ones? And if what he says is true, how can he be so cruel to a bunch of widowers, orphans and parents who just lost their little children? How could they outright kill all these people who didn't pass the selection? Trainloads of people! We would've surely heard some gunfire. Nah! The smoke and the stench are from corpses of those who died on the train or in the barracks. Why the cruelty? Our own Jews! Even if they're low-lives, as Jews, they are supposed to show some humanity!

He's finally finished baiting us and another much smaller kapo takes over the "welcoming". He walks before us on a long stage-like projection so that we can all see him and introduces himself in Yiddish as the "*Kishivmacher* (a wizard, a magician)", a nickname, he says, earned through his rare ability to produce jewelry, gold and cash out of those who claim not to have any. He paces before us, intoning his words monotonously, patiently, as if trying to hypnotize us: "Surrender all your valuables to me, and I'll see that you receive special privileges. It's pointless for you to hang on to your valuables in here. It is also a great crime. You'll be found out and dreadful consequences will await you. By law, your possessions are the property of the German Reich."

He suddenly stops and ominously raises his index finger. He stares at us forcefully and quizzically: "Did you hear that gunshot outside? Did you?" I make a quick mental note that I didn't, although he's so persuasive that I'm willing to agree that, indeed, I did. "Surely, you must have heard it," he continues. "I'll let you guess what that was, eh?! Yeah, that shot just put an end to someone who tried to hide his valuables. So make your choice now. Do you want to live here and have all kinds of privileges, or do you want to end up like that guy who has just been shot dead?" He looks intensely at each and every one of us as if convinced that we are concealing something of value. Just where are we supposed to hide something when everything was already taken away from us, our rectums thoroughly checked, and gold teeth knocked out from those who had them? Where does this joker-wizard think we could be hiding something unless we had swallowed it and keep it now in our bellies? I look in bewilderment at the other new arrivals, but they seem to be just as perplexed. But the *Kishivmacher* isn't giving up: "If at least one of you doesn't surrender his hidden valuables, you'll be standing here all day without any food. And a delicious soup is being distributed right now. Can you smell it?" he concludes.

Our men haven't eaten in three days, and surely every one of us would pull out his own teeth and hand it over to the *Kishivmacher* for a few spoonfuls of that "delicious soup." But the wizard's witchcraft isn't producing any valuables. No one here has a single thing to declare. The magician's spell has failed, and we may be deprived of that "delicious soup" after all.

Chapter 15:
To Work or Not to Work

The welcoming is finally over and we're allowed to return to our barrack. It's time for our midday feeding, and we welcome the sight of a caldron with soup. We form a line, and expectantly walk up with our bowls to the ladlers. We weren't given any spoons, but there are no solids in our soup anyway. The privileged ones get the solid contents. For us, the kitchen workers scoop it from the top but dig deep for more nourishing morsels when they know someone personally or when barrack functionaries get theirs. After the ghetto years, we're familiar with favoritism. I drink the watery soup out of my tin bowl and watch how the others wolf it down, then get in line for seconds. There's a stir at the caldron, and the kapos thrash their clubs right and left to keep order. I stay away to avoid a clubbing; anyway I'm not as starved as the others because I had rice and milk yesterday.

We're allowed to walk on the "promenade", a simple dirt walkway that runs between the row of barracks. Four rows of electrically charged barbed wires isolate our camp from the women's. We'd like to get near them to find out about our female relatives, but the tower-guard may fire at us. My thoughts go to Mama and then to Aunt Hela, and I sigh with relief that at least she remained in the ghetto. How are she and Sym evading the Hitlerites? Hours pass as we drift gaping at thousands of gaunt, strange faces.

Towards evening we get a slice of bread with a sliver of sausage, which the starved men wolf down on the spot. Soon we'll have evening assembly, so we stay near our barrack for fear of getting lost in this vast city of identical barracks. Showing up late for Appell is severely punished, and we also try to limit walking, to conserve our energy.

Again we spend the night on a crowded floor. But we're so weak that we don't even react when the others lay their arms, legs or heads on us. The second morning in the camp is the same as the first: reveille around 4 a.m. to the muffled and mournful *Aufstehen* instantly followed by dreadful clubbing – a methodical, dutiful thrashing of bodies still on the concrete floor – only this time, some men can't even duck the blows.

Again we spend some hours in the dark, all bunched up, shivering and clinging to each other for a bit of warmth. Those seemingly dead get dragged outside and left in front of the barrack for the morning count, which is very high. We watch the grim harvest of seemingly lifeless bodies being dragged out for roll call and body count and some men mutter the unthinkable: "Who knows if they are not better off than us?"

The kapos are our direct bane. They maim and murder at will and show no regard for our older men, telling them brutally: "If you're fifty, you've lived long enough." One of their "exercises" is so hard on these "elders" that many collapse during it. They make us squat very slowly with bent knees and outstretched arms. This strains our leg muscles; older men who can't do it slowly, squat and rise quickly, for which they are mercilessly beaten. This cruel drill weeds out the frail, the awkward, and, most of all, the elderly, who somehow slipped in through the selection on arrival.

"Look, if you don't like it here, you don't have to take any of this," our *Blockaelteste* (Barrack Chief) tells us at assembly. "No one is forcing you to stay here. See those wires? Just run up at them. A few from your transport already did so. Go ahead! Be my guest. Enjoy!" These thugs are really witty. Huge, beefy, stocky, overbearing, well-fed – surely from siphoning our thousands of rations – they act like petty despots of their principalities. And they try to find amusement in everything, including their malicious euphemisms. Although, the Barrack Boss goading us to commit suicide at the high-powered wires may not even be sarcastic. Maybe opting for a quick death *is* better than lingering in this Hellhole. They don't make much of a fuss over human life in here. And yet, we still don't want to believe that so many who arrived with us are no more. I dare not think of murder on such a scale. But the oppressive and continuous stench makes us wonder – what kind of industry do they have here that so many thousands of us were needed?

Although the smoke heads upwards, the foul stench nauseates and gags me as it envelops us all like an invisible fog. Is this smoke really what's left of our relatives, our reward for slave labor? Those kapos surely were kidding with their "your relatives are going up with the smoke." A cruel joke! How can we even consider it seriously? Their sadistic bating destroys any flicker of our hope. There's no light at the end of the tunnel. The tunnel is converging. It's almost a coffin.

Surely the SS here have no more love for the brutish kapos than for the rest of us. But so long as they need their grisly services, they suspend their loathing for these killers. And the kapos surely know it, but yet are ready to take our lives – their brethren – just to prolong their own if only for a short time. Is the human instinct to live so overwhelming that we're capable of wanton killings just to save our own necks for another day?

Before the evening roll-call, we're moved from Barrack #25 to Barrack #12, which is identical. The Barrack Boss is a tall, brawny Polish Jew. He addresses us arrogantly in flawed German that is more Yiddish than German: "There's going to be order in my barrack, or I myself will punish each and every one of you." And he twists his huge, sinewy hands as if wringing a wet cloth. He's just another gruff brute. His evident Jewishness won't do us any good. This hellhole neutralizes one's background, ethnicity and refined upbringing. In the ghetto, too, there were Jewish policemen who stemmed from well-bred families, but routed Jews up, beating them in the process. Here, in addition to beatings, these kapos take sadistic pleasure in destroying any flicker of our hope.

We spend another night on the concrete floor just as crowded as in the previous barrack. I dream that I'm back on the dragon-train and can even sense its hypnotic staccato beat… I wake up with a feeling of abysmal emptiness. Everybody here must feel abandoned and desolate. No one talks to each other, but suffers in silence the noticeable absence of women and children. Each man is like a burned-out shell of unrelieved homesickness.

Why are the kapos so secretive about the fate of those who were not selected for work? What are all those cryptic allusions to the smoke as the "heavenly highway"? Why don't they tell us if those selected on arrival were really killed and how?

"*Aufstehen, aufstehen, los, los!* (Up, up, go, go!)" Again, I hear those insidiously muffled voices of the kapos and the thud of their bats, cracking skulls and breaking bones. Shouts of pain and impotent outrage only provoke the kapos more. The gigantic Jewish Barrack Boss towers over everything, distributing blows right and left, methodically, indiscriminately, unhurriedly, as if performing a routine exercise in the field, like thrashing wheat.

Then another two chilly hours of standing like a herd of cows in the pre-dawn darkness and mulling over the fate of our loved ones. What will this new day bring us – liberation or death? Or "liberation through death" as the kapos tell us. Will we be sent to some kind of work? Up to now, the Germans have used us for two kinds of labor: real productive work, or just an exercise in humiliation not connected with any German needs. They did this in the beginning of their occupation when they caught Jews in the street, loaded them onto trucks, then took them to public places like city boulevards to scrub pavements or clean public toilets with their bare hands and remove feces with their own shirts or blouses, jeering them with such comments as: "At last we put the Jews to work."

Now, however, they may have a third kind of work for us; entirely aimless except for killing the laborers. I saw it from the train, on arrival, where men carried huge rocks to and fro. Why would the Germans, so in need of manual or skilled manpower, waste it while it would be so much more practical having us clear rubble from their bombed out cities or tend their factories and agricultural fields?

There is a stir on the promenade: a kapo is looking for masons and carpenters. Dozens of inmates rush over for work. Stagnating in this transitory camp means that one's days are numbered and that we may indeed last no longer than a week. In a real labor camp, maybe one could stretch those days. Here we'll surely wither through starvation, sleep deprivation, or be clubbed to death by the kapos. It's worth a try to volunteer for work. But the work-kapo, a stodgy Pole named Tadek, warns us that he's looking only for experts in certain fields. "Anyone who turns out to be a fraud will be dealt with mercilessly." Several men who stepped up have second thoughts and retreat hastily. Those who stick it out are tested. The squatty Tadek asks them a few questions, and then selects those who answer correctly. A couple of scribes who assist him jot down the inmates' numbers. The chosen men seem glad. There may be hope to get away from this hellhole, though the chances look slim, since only a dozen men were chosen from thousands. But even this slim hope gives us a renewed will to survive.

"Don't think work will save you," mutters an older man. "You may get a little more food, but you'll use up much more energy. And the guards sometimes amuse themselves with cruel games. They'll snatch the cap off your head and toss it towards the wires, telling you to fetch it, then shoot you when you go after it. Then they'll report it as an escape attempt, and even get some schnapps for it. If you refuse to fetch, they'll shoot you for disobedience. Think about it. Don't aid their war effort by being productive."

So now what? To work or not to work? Getting out of here presents some hope but staying means facing the wrenching hunger. It's also important to stay healthy. "*Ein Laus, dein Tod* (A louse is your death)," warn the posters around the camp to promote cleanliness and prevent infectious disease. Yet no soap is provided, no hot water, no towels and no change of clothing. I heard that when an SS camp doctor once found a barrack having a continuous problem with lice, he ordered everybody in it killed. So that's the true meaning of that poster: That deadly louse is an SS *doctor*!

Chapter 16:
Two Uncles

I continue to drift down the promenade and notice two shabby-looking men, one tall, one short, standing together and watching me intently. The shorter one looks even smaller in his oversized stripes. I instantly recognize Uncle Heniek by his characteristic A-shaped eyebrows. Heniek Wolborski, the shrewd and once prosperous businessman, always fashionably dressed and smelling of nice cologne, now looks like a strayed little tramp in this oversize zebra jacket and pants creased like an accordion below his knees. Even in the ghetto he was wheeling and dealing and providing for Aunt Asta and their two daughters. With him is Uncle Ignatz, his brother-in-law, who looks just as forlorn without Aunt Andzia and their two daughters. Should I walk over and commiserate with them on their women and their probable fate? It can't be a happy reunion without their wives and daughters whom I love so dearly.

Slowly, apprehensively, I approach them, not quite sure what to say or how to act. First, the Germans stripped us of our homes and businesses, and now they also took our loved ones. As I look at them, my thoughts are with their families: Heniek's wife, Aunt Asta, and their cute little eleven-year-old, pug-face Lilka, and the older Stefa, who, at the time of evacuation, was in the ghetto hospital with something and was probably shipped out with the rest of the patients; and Ignatz's wife, Aunt Andzia, and their two daughters, the adorable ten-year-old Rysia, and the quiet twelve-year-old Gizia. Both Asta and Andzia, Mama's younger sisters, always treated me with love and care. To see their husbands without them is eerie. I know that my aunts would never let the SS separate

them from their little darlings even if they knew that they had to die with
them.

I recall that Uncle Heniek told us in the last few days in the ghetto
that we would be sent to Auschwitz. Surely he wasn't aware of the true nature of this horror-camp. But how could he know what goes on in here?
No German official would reveal to him or to anyone what really goes on
in here. And what if we had known? Then what? Would we have hidden
in a cellar and wait for the Red Army to liberate us, taking a chance of
being discovered and killed? Surely, yes, if we had known then what we
only suspect now.

As I approach them, I notice that they're looking at me oddly; Uncle
Heniek with his hands in the pockets of those clownish pants, callous-
ly nodding his chin in my direction and commenting to Uncle Ignatz:
"Those of his age stand the best chance of surviving in here." Uncle Ignatz
nods in assent. His pale blue eyes are fixated on my shoes that he gave me
a few days before deportation. It was a blessing that I got to wear them
instead of my bottomless, make-shift pair.

Responding to his stare, I look at his feet only to discover them shod
in an ungainly pair of clogs. So that's it! Some kapo must have taken those
conspicuous, beautiful brand new black riding boots and given him these
sorrowful clogs instead. Now he'd surely like to have his old shoes back
from me in exchange for these cumbersome clogs. His intensive stare
makes me feel extremely uneasy.

They haven't said one word to me, but enviously keep staring at
me and my shoes. Aghast, I freeze and flinch. Slowly, without a word, I
begin to withdraw, inching backwards and let the milling inmates surge
in between us. I'm pained and sullen that my opportunity to bond with
my two uncles and bemoan the fate of our lost female relatives has come
to naught. Moreover, I feel culpable for the possession of the shoes, my
sole property besides my belt – the only two things that weren't taken
from me. There are finally enough men traipsing between us, and I turn
around and walk away, losing myself in the crowd. And yet, even with all
these men between us, I can still feel Uncle Ignatz's piercing glare fixated
on my shoes.

I feel wretched. Here, in this miserable camp, my two uncles are *en-
vying me*! One envies my youth and the other my shoes. Uncle Heniek's
comment that the young have the best chance to survive here makes me
realize that Mama may be doomed, even though her last words, "I'm with
the young," were meant to encourage me.

I must distance myself from this painful encounter. How could these
two men, clever, intelligent, prudent and politically astute, let themselves

be trapped with their wives and daughters in this no-exit hell-hole? They had the foresight to analyze and even correctly predict Hitler's moves before he waged war on Poland, but they couldn't for the life of them evade their own impending doom. Shouldn't they have taken their families, during the so-called ghetto dissolution, and crawl into some hole and stay in it for days even at the risk of starving to death rather than trust the German promises that "families will stay together"? Now they're in this death-camp, probably widowed and childless, after all those years of their devoted fatherhood. Even if they themselves manage to survive against all odds, how will they be able to go through life without their lovely wives and daughters?

I must try to forget my encounter with them. To retain my sanity, I must rid myself of all emotional ties. Just as the kapos stripped me of my personal belongings, I must now free my mind of any depressing feelings as well. I must desensitize myself to the goings-on in here and live as if suspended in nothingness.

Chapter 17:
Postmortems

The milling crowd fills the space between me and my two uncles. The bad encounter will make me avoid them unless we reunite with Mama's sisters someday.

At once, I recognize a couple of boys with whom I worked in the Electro-technical Workshop. Both are ardent communists: Felek Lipinski is a cool-headed and rational boy, while Lolek Aksztein is a bellicose hot-head, who beat up the boss's son on the floor of the plant. They nod to me coolly – I never attended their gatherings – and continue talking about the inevitable victory of communism over fascism, as if they were still in the shop. I'm surprised at their stamina to argue on empty stomachs, but their passionate idealism is hard to contain. Talking may even be good, as it distracts attention from hunger. I warn them that such talk will cause trouble here, but they carry on. Maybe I should keep away. If someone reports them to the SS, we'll all get punished. But I stay on. With them, I have the illusion that we are still in the ghetto and soon we'll go home to our doting mothers.

I share with them my witnessing Rozenblat's torture and Moishe Husyd's boast of murdering Rumek while comforting us with, "Your tormentor is gone."

"The fascist dogs had it coming for thier collaboration," Lolek flares up.

"Rumek tried to prevent a bloodbath by cooperation," Felek says, "always concerned with sparing the ghetto as a whole and proving that we could be productive and vital to the German economy. Who could foresee that after all our slave labor, we'd wind up here?"

"Sure, and that's how they got us," Lolek counters. "Always reassuring us that we'd be spared if we only got rid of the "excess burden": the sick, the aged, the unproductive."

"And we always reasoned that we wouldn't be among them," Felek says.

"He sold his soul to the devil," Lolek insists.

"Which many of us would do if only given a chance," Felek observes.

"I thought of striking a bargain with the devil two days ago," I say. "When Biebow[1] was accompanying the SS to rout us for deportation. I thought of offering him my treasured stamp collection for letting me and my mother remain in the ghetto."

Lolek snickers: "And then he'd bow and thank you for your generous offer, yet decline such a treasured possession. But he'd let you, your mother, and all your other relatives remain in the ghetto for as long as you want anyway. And then, he'd invite you home for dinner to show off such a rare specimen of a gutsy Jew-boy to his family."

Felek is less sarcastic: "He'd lay you out cold before you could even hand him your album. He shot others to death that approached him with pleadings during evacuation."

"But what if he didn't? Wouldn't that be just like striking a deal with the devil?" I asked.

"Not a chance," Felek objects. "Even if he were an ardent philatelist or even if you handed him a fortune in gold and jewelry, he wouldn't take it in the presence of the SS. Accepting a gift from a nervy Jew-boy who tempts his Aryan integrity? No way!"

"But what about the purity of my motive? Remaining in a dissolved ghetto with my mother surely wouldn't upset the grand scheme of the Nazi world conquest," I added.

"The purity of anything coming from you is voided by your being a filthy Jew in his eyes, a bag of shit. You've got no innocence, no purity, no morals. You're wretched, damned, and evil. The Nazis are doing the world a service by eliminating the likes of you," Felek rattles off these hackneyed Nazi phrases.

Arguing has never been more exhausting. Talking about our relatives' fate will have to wait. I'm trembling with anticipation as I head for my barrack to get in line for the long-awaited first meal – the mid-day soup.

---

1   Hans Biebow, Chief Nazi Administrator of the Litzmannstadt Ghetto

Chapter 18:
Trampling a Musulman

S till without a spoon, I greedily, voraciously, ravenously, swallow the watery soup in huge gulps, then pick up the three thin slices of potato left in the bottom of my bowl and, like some exquisite dessert, chew them very slowly to prolong the process of eating.

When all in our barrack are served, they start doling out seconds. The men shove, push, fall, fight, crawl and bite just to get near the cauldron. This seething and snapping makes us look like animals. Hunger releases such animalistic aggression that it makes one wonder about man's claim to have been created in the image of God. This feeding frenzy must surely convince the SS that we are indeed subhuman and deserving contempt along with any abuse they see fit for us. I don't try to go for seconds; even if I'm lucky enough to get it, these few mouthfuls would hardly replenish the energy lost on my struggle.

For this extra bit of soup, some inmates shove and fight anybody, even their own fathers or sons, showing no pity on anyone. The hunger, the overcrowding, and the abuse from the kapos make us extremely irritable and aggressive, and we constantly snap at each other. Cut off from our women and other close relatives, and unaware of their fate, many become apathetic at such callous acts of cruelty and brutality. Maybe it's better this way. Emotional involvement requires an input of energy, which we're already sapped of.

As the kitchen workers are done with their soup distribution and ready to haul off their cauldron, one inmate dives headlong into it, causing them to drop it with a loud crash. He is now half inside of it and keeps scooping up the sediment. An SS officer who happens to be swaggering by, notices the commotion, and shouts: "*Du verfluchte Drecksack! Ich werde dir mahl ein bisschen Ordnung zeigen!* (You accursed pile of shit! I'm going to show you some order in here!)"

In an instant, the inmates scatter away, but the Musulman[1], a tall, frail shadow of a man, oblivious to the world around him, keeps scooping scraps of food off the cauldron walls and licking them off his spoon. The officer drags him out by the collar of his jacket, lifts him from behind, and whacks him across his ghostly face, knocking him off his feet. But the sack-of-bones Musulman who tumbles next to the cauldron on the ground doesn't give up: with eyes of a crazed animal, looking wild and to the side, he disregards the indignant SS officer towering over him, and thrusts his hand – still grasping the spoon – back into the cauldron, scrapes the sediment, and greedily licks it off. The officer now kicks him in the ribs. The pitiful skeleton rolls over from the impact but still holds on to the rim of the cauldron with one hand while shoving the spoon into his mouth with the other. The German, with ever-increasing effort, kicks and kicks again, aiming his shiny black riding boots at the kidneys, equally determined to dislodge the man from inside the cauldron. But the wretched, bony body just quivers from the impact, while the hand still scrapes and the mouth licks, scrapes and licks, scrapes and licks…

"*Wozu willst du noch leben?* (Why do you still want to go on living?)" shouts the officer almost out of breath. "*Zu scheissen noch ein Tag?* (To go on shitting for another day?)" He stops the kicking. He gasps and tries to catch his breath, then sputters: "To foul up the air with your filthy Jewish shit, you swine!" He's visibly amused at the man's obstinacy and shakes his head incredulously – maybe in disgust – then delivers one powerful kick to the back, as if to test the man's desperate tenacity. A clank in the kettle indicates that the man dropped his spoon. But his scooping motions don't stop. He is now wiping the cauldron walls either with his fingers or with his hands. The upper half of his torso is inside. He bends his knees as if trying to crawl completely inside to evade the punishing kicks and to be closer to the life-saving soup scraps. But the German kicks again and again, deliberately, unhurriedly, and without anger, driving the pointed tip of his boot into the man's back near the kidneys. Each time the bony body just twitches.

"*Komm 'mal 'raus, du Drecksack! 'Raus mit dir!* (Come out, you pile of shit! Out with you!)" The officer's voice is now strained as he gasps for breath, but the man in the cauldron just goes on lapping up the

---

1   The SS men used this term as a funny expression to describe completely emaciated, zombie-like apparitions.

wall, probably unaware that his tormentor is an SS officer. The German nudges the man with his foot to flatten him, and then jumps onto his exposed belly again and again, as if to squeeze the bits of food back out of him. The Musulman is so skinny that his paper-thin belly may snap under the weight of the jumping SS man. And yet, he goes on scraping, lying on his back. The officer steps off the man's belly and tramples it now with one foot, stamping and grinding his spiked boot until the man is motionless.

Finally the spectacle is over. The man's legs stiffen; his upper body is still inside the cauldron. The officer orders the kitchen workers to carry on and, without even checking if his victim is dead, struts away with his characteristic swagger, apparently pleased with himself that he managed to restore some order in this chaotic place. The kitchen workers drag the Musulman out of their cauldron, leave him lying on the ground, then toss out his spoon near him. A few men make a dash for it. The ladlers disappear with their cauldron. The rest of us carry on as if nothing extraordinary has happened, apparently getting more accustomed to wanton acts of murder. No one even checks if the hapless Musulman is still breathing. Death is all the more final because, unlike in the ghetto, where proper rites and individual graves served as a person's final resting place, here one is turned into smoke without leaving a tangible trace or even any record of his death.

Stamping on people seems to be the preferred way of murder in here, human beings treated like noxious bugs to be squashed under a shoe, too odious to even lay one's hands on. And yet, even when squashing a bug, one is expected to display some revulsion, but this SS officer showed only surprise at his victim's tenacity, while meting out his punishment methodically without a scowl, anger or overt sadism. The SS men keep indulging their aggression with total disregard for the pain they cause and without any fear of possible reprisals. Such wanton destructiveness probably gives them a feeling of omnipotence and mastery over nature. By extinguishing life they must feel that they are in control of it. Their indifference to suffering and death makes them veritable monsters. They only look human. It's ironic that moviemakers feel it necessary to portray their fictional monsters as physically deformed and with ghoulish faces, whereas truly evil men appear as normal-looking as these stolid and probably church-going and "God-fearing" German burghers in their SS uniforms.

Chapter 19:
In Limbo

S huffling along on the busy promenade, I try to meet the two boys from the ghetto who, unlike my two uncles, won't begrudge me my youth or my shoes. I find them near their barrack and relate the SS officer's murder of the Musulman. Lolek mutters some predictable Marxist platitude about a fascist flunky produced by a decadent capitalistic system. Felek muses that wanton killing is a diversion here for those who can get away with it and may be a revolt against God: "Hitler told his followers to return to barbarism and throw off the shackles of civilization to feel free of morals and of conscience, which, he claims, is a Jewish invention. Such killings make the SS feel in control of life and of death as if they were a powerful deity themselves."

There's a feverish activity nearby. We push ourselves into the crowd and become separated. They're recruiting inmates for work outside of Auschwitz. The same Polish kapo, Tadek, is looking for skilled carpenters and masons only. But those constitute a very small percentage of our arrivals. He questions some men who step forward. I drift away disappointed that he didn't ask for electricians. We'll be doomed without getting on a work crew. The men are also dejected because of having lost their families, wondering what was done with all those who didn't pass the selection. Maybe the wise Felek knows more than I do about this, but his logical deduction would only confirm my worst fears. If the life of an able-bodied man is of no value in here, what possible use can they have for the frail, the elderly and the children whom they took from us on arrival?

WHACK!! A resounding blow to my head sends me reeling. "*Da hasst du eine Backfeife in die Fresse damit du aufpasst wohin du gehst, du Drecksack!* (Here's a smack in your puss, so that you watch where you go, you bag o'shit!)" Instinctively my hand goes up to my pummeled ear to rub a stinging and burning as I try to keep from falling down. A rather slight inmate hit me and I wonder why. He wears close-fitting zebra stripes, apparently tailor-made and his cap is jauntily cocked. He has a pink triangle of a homosexual on his uniform. He's self-assured and speaks with an Austrian dialect.

"*Halt die Goschn, du Trottle, du!* (Shut your trap, you ninny!)", he adds quickly as I'm about to say something in protest. Why did he whack me? I didn't bump him or even brush against him.

"*Na, los! Schiess im Wind!* (Beat it! Get lost!)", he adds in passing as he briskly walks away, raising himself on tiptoes with each elastic step as if bouncing on a springboard.

I rub my sore ear as he disappears in the crowd. Maybe I didn't get out of his way fast enough. Some privileged dandy! His bouncy gait is what makes these prominents so different from the rest of us. It's as if they were about to leap up in the air and take off flying. What bubbling energy it takes to rebound like that! The German soldiers walk with a strut called the goose-step; these bastards here, walk – nay, prance – on spring coils; and we can barely drag our feet, even when we don't wear those clumsy clogs.

We are being punished as Jews – a crime that surpasses all others. But why are we branded as "political"? We are not here for our political leanings, felonies or even civil disobedience, but just for being Jewish. Just for being alive!

I shuffle toward my barrack. Maybe it's time for the evening bread. I'm edgy like a zoo beast at feeding time. How many days have I been here already? Are my two weeks of life up yet? My memory is slipping. But no bread yet…must occupy my mind with something. Maybe talk to the two boys and take my mind off the hunger pains.

Chapter 20:
A Piece of Bread for Mama

Too exhausted to continue the talk, I return to my barrack. They finally distribute the evening ration: a piece of bread and a sliver of margarine. I'm looking at the portion in my hand. My hunger is dulled now. Should I save it for later when hunger tugs at my entrails again or eat it now and be done with it? What's inside of me is mine. As the camp saying goes: No one can pilfer what's in my belly. What to do? I could have given it to Mama if she were with me – to repay her at least partially for all that she's done for me before it's too late.

But the women are in another section of the vast camp and isolated by high-powered barbed wire. And there must be thousands of women. Finding Mama would be nearly impossible even if I could get into the women's camp.

Suddenly I'm aware of a cavernous abyss in my stomach. It tears at my innards, roaring in anger like a lion that's being kept from feeding on his catch. I take a small bite of the bread and margarine and try to chew it very slowly and mix it with saliva before it plops down into that Moloch of a stomach. I'm still thinking of saving most of the bread for Mama, though I'm not at all sure how I would be able to send it to her.

After chewing it for a long time and savoring the bliss of a mouth filled with food, I swallow the first morsel. But instead of being appeased, my stomach roars for more. I take another small bite with the good intention that sharing even a half ration with Mama would do her good and make *me* feel good. She's surely having the same thoughts while nibbling on her ration in the women's camp. I chew and chew, salivating to add bulk, delaying the swallowing and letting the nourishing juices soothe my stomach.

At last I swallow the second morsel, but my stomach still isn't appeased. It clamors for more. I take a third small bite, still thinking of Mama. I masticate with an overpowering feeling of guilt as I see myself sitting at our table in the ghetto, nibbling slowly away a whole weekly ration of bread for Mama and me, with the same self-reproach that I'm going through now. But I chew on, and on, and on. I take another small bite. And chew, and chew, and swallow, and bite again, and chew, and again. And the bread and margarine that were to last a full twenty-four hours until tomorrow evening – are gone. It will now be really hard to last till the next feeding.

Chapter 21:
A Selection in Here

Another night in the crammed barrack, but now with more room on the floor, we can sit and even lie without cramping others. The barrack kapos are disposing of us with great swiftness. Are they making room for new arrivals? But from where? Our transport from the ghetto was the last. All the Jews from villages and towns around Lodz were sent to our ghetto long ago, which was also the last stop for Czechoslovakian, Hungarian and Austrian Jews. Are there Jews left in Europe whom the Hitlerites haven't rounded up yet?

Again the muffled morning *"Aufstehen!"* with skull-cracking clubs to which we respond with an eerie chorus of moans, groans and cries of outrage. This circus of cruelty is fun for these killer-kapos – an arena for their deception, power and prowess.

Again we stand outside in silence, huddled in the chill of a dark pre-dawn. Propped up by neighbors, we continue sleeping. The dead or dying are dragged out and laid out in front of the barrack. Some men, in utter despair, dare to report for "Krankenbau", the medical building. Surely they're too sick to stand up and too resigned to even consider that to the Germans, a sick Jew or one in need of medical attention, may be a dead Jew.

We're retaining our bodily functions until the trip to the latrine. But this will come only after the morning Appell, then the "coffee". But the roll-call is late and the sun is already up. Finally we assemble on the square in front of our barrack. The kapos drill us in how to form ranks and in snapping off our caps to the command *"Muetzen ab!"*

Finally an SS officer takes the count and exits. But we are not dismissed. Maybe the numbers don't add up. We stand at attention for a long time. At once, they order us to spread out so that there's more space between the rows. "*Los! Schnell!* Take everything off!" The command to strip naked except for our footwear is new and odd. "Everything," means only the jacket and pants for we've no shirts, underwear, or socks.

"Put your pants in front of you! Fold your jacket over your arm so that your number is clearly visible!" We carry out this unusual command and stand shivering in the chilly morning air. A barrage of piercing whistles indicates that the whole camp is under a special curfew. Something important is afoot. Maybe it is an inspection for lice or an infectious disease? But it drags on and on. Some men can't stand up any longer and collapse. Those next to them try to prop them up because the kapos kick the fallen ones so vehemently that some won't ever stand up again; then they are dragged off to the front of the assembly and left on the ground for the count. We surely must all think the same: if we could only get through this new ordeal, we'll persevere. All atrocities in here seem to have a similar effect on us: if I just survive this one, I may yet live to see the end of my travails, and if not the end – at least to just live for another day.

"*Achtung! Augen rechts!* (Attention! Eyes to the right!)", the shrill commands pierce the cold air with the same menacing urgency that we heard in the cattle-cars on arrival. Instantly we stick out our bare chests and suck in our stomachs in military fashion. I notice several SS officers with a retinue of soldiers in helmets and rifles at-the-ready, all briskly entering the square in front of our barrack. We stand rigid, trying not to shake from the cold air and from fear, but our emaciated muscles keep twitching frantically under our pale skin to generate warmth. I visualize a horse, flittering its rump skin to shake off bothersome gnats.

The SS officers walk slowly between our rows, scrutinizing each inmate's body. Occasionally they order the man to turn around, then take a closer look at his posterior. Then they order an assisting scribe to jot down the man's number.

SELECTION!! OH, NO! We pass this dreaded word among us in a whisper, but it has the effect of a thunderclap striking into our midst. The morning Appell has turned into Judgment Day – another doomsday selection, a repeat of the one on arrival, with Mama's "I'm with the young," still reverberating in my head. Already cold from the morning chill, our naked, emaciated bodies now shake quite visibly and our teeth chatter aloud. We present a sorry sight, as for the most part we're reduced to skin and bones. Even the flesh of our buttocks is so pitifully decreased that the pelvis is clearly defined. By just looking at an inmate's arse, the

SS determine if a man is a candidate for the junk heap. A wasted rump in here indicates an inmate's exclusion from joining a work crew, hence from the human race. First they starve us to a complete atrophy, and then, when we're skeletal, they send us off to "go up with the smoke," as the kapos hinted.

A flash from the past stirs my memory – another irony: In the outdoor Green Market in Lodz before the war, I saw women shoppers blow the feathers on a live chicken's arse, to see if it was worth buying; namely, if it was sufficiently fat for cooking and for rendering cracklings – a delicacy I used to eat hot or smeared on bread together with the tasty chicken fat. If the chicken wasn't fat enough, the women didn't buy it and its life was spared. But a skinny arse in here assures a swift passage to death.

Our great relief at passing the Selection at the depot four days ago has, alas, come to an end. And we thought that we had won a new lease on life then, but apparently not for long. A sunken buttocks equates to a collapsed universe. These seemingly insignificant parts of a man's anatomy now determine if he's to continue living or to die – just like the hapless chickens in the Lodz Green Market. Why don't these goons here look into a man's face and into his eyes and search for some spirit and his resolve to live? Full, fleshy buttocks – that's our sole value for the SS!

In spite of our terror, we stand stiffly drawn, trying not to reveal any emotions, especially of weakness. We avoid looking directly at them even when answering questions. The Selection proceeds very slowly. They don't want to miss anyone fit to be weeded out. The good old Germans are well known for their thoroughness.

I wonder how my buttocks look. Trying not to attract attention, I slide my right hand from my thigh, against which it is flattened in my rigid attention stance, and toward my behind. Does it have enough flesh to let me "pass"? Thank God I'm not yet a Musulman ready for the "junk heap", though it's difficult to feel reassured when one's life depends on the whimsy of the omnipotent SS.

I conjure billiard balls that some still rounded buttocks remind me of in contrast to those hopelessly withered. Bright orbs rebounding off the rails of a huge green billiard table in a room of hushed spectators. The expert player with his cue, like with a magic wand, controls the seemingly intractable motion of three wondrous balls, sending the one which he stroked toward its target, spinning, rebounding, caroming... and that final turn and click on impact. Score! Is this just a game or a Grand Cosmic Plan for the Motion of Spheres? When Dad, before the war, took me along to a cafe where he met people on business, I had a chance to watch these rolling spheres on their convoluted orbits, as they sometimes even reversed directions in mid-course like they were controlled by a higher power. Were the players trying to emulate the Great-Technician-Up-There who launched it all at the onset of His Creation? Perhaps Man's attempts at grasping divinity turn up when he can bend the laws of physics to his whimsical will and be the master of his own fate.

It's over at last! The SS are withdrawing; they got their numbers, surely pleased with themselves for a job well done. We don the jacket and pants on our shivering bodies and line up for morning "coffee". We're too shaken up to even talk or look at each other. How do you act or what do you say to someone whose number was written down and who's now destined for certain death? It's very depressing to realize that the dreaded selections take place even in here and that our own emaciated bodies may mark us for the end.

The whole camp is as if in mourning. No one is talking. The men hover like specters. Even hunger isn't as oppressive when death is imminent. At evening Appell, they call out the numbers of those who didn't pass the Selection. Some, tearfully, bid their relatives or friends farewell. A contingent of SS men, with rifles at-the-ready, makes sure that each and every one of them is promptly marched out of our row of barracks.

Chapter 22:
The Wilderness

There's more room tonight on the barrack floor after yesterday's Selection. For the first time in days, I'm able to lie on the concrete floor without touching anyone. The barrack kapos wake us in their usual way by cracking skulls and bones. We are too slow to evade their crushing cudgels as they chase us out of the barrack into a dark chill. Drowsy and hungry, we shiver, huddling for warmth in a huge circle.

I pray for a faster arrival of dawn: Come out already and shine on us oh mighty sun! Slowly the mountain peaks emerge on the horizon, projecting skyward their tall pines like church steeples. Their luxurious forests are surely carpeted with dense, soft moss, creating a hushed tranquility for anything that treads on its spongy flooring. I see myself walking on it and singing praises to the Great Creator of such a beautiful nature. Ah, if I could only stretch out on that gentle moss and admire the swift brooks, the solemn, majestic firs, plush meadows...and inhale the intoxicating fragrance of forest vegetation, where even decay releases its own redolent fragrance...all so close and yet so remote beyond high-voltage wires, guard-towers, the SS and their murderous servant-kapos. The lush nature, so near, may as well be on a photo. Ah, the wilderness, the pristine forests, the country-side, the quaint Polish villages with their ever present sculptures of Christ on the cross; That Jesus who was born, lived, and died in his Jewish homeland in Judea, is accepted by Poles as their own, while his brethren descendants are regarded as aliens, unwelcome outsiders, even though they've dwelt on this Polish soil for one-thousand years and bled for it in its struggles for independence.

God created this "wilderness" as a thin strip of land on which to make our existence, suspended between the earth's deep core and the unfathomable space above. As in those two immense physical layers, we are also suspended between the temporal ones, existing in the narrow confine of the present. The past is dead, vivid only in memory; the future, like the space above us, is mysterious, distant and uncertain. Will it shower us with sunshine or with meteors? We can only control the present. Or can we?

We keep inhaling the nauseating stench from smoldering fumes of the billowy smoke that climbs skywards from towering stacks, soaking us all in its noxious vapors. What industry makes the Germans incinerate here day and night, rubber for tires or...?

I was scared as a child by the fairy tale of Hansel and Gretel as the old hag tries to shove them into flames. But she winds up in her own oven. The children survive and are reunited with their parents. It was only a fable, but now?! Could this nightmarish fairy tale be real and even multiplied a thousand-fold in our factual, non-fictional lives...?

And out there, in those woods, lies the so-called "wilderness". What do we have here then? It must be "civilization"!

Chapter 23:
The Air Raid

T he morning passes as usual: "*Appell, Kafe, Scheisshaus* (Assembly, coffee, shithouse)", then we drift aimlessly between the barracks, hoping to join an "Arbeitskommando (Work-crew)", which could mean an extra ration of soup or bread. Some men, fearful of losing their last bit of energy on physical effort, don't even look for work, suspecting that the SS are trying to work us to death. I'm looking for my two acquaintances to see if they survived the Selection. Even if we were spared this time, in a few days our eyes will sink in, flesh will vanish, and only skin will cover our protruding bones…and then what?

SHRIEK! A sudden shrill cry of a wailing siren slashes through the camp air, then frantic whistles and hysterical commands: "*Los, los, in die Barracken! Los, los, schnell!* (Move, move into the barracks! Move, move fast!)" It's an air-raid alarm. Is it possible? The allies are here?! They can penetrate the defenses of the mighty Luftwaffe all the way to this fortress of death, this grisly Murderopolis?!

Pandemonium breaks out. SS men run, whistle, shout. They urge us to take cover in the nearest barrack. Quickly! "*Los, los!*" I'm delirious. The SS are urging us to save *our* lives?! What an unexpected cacophony of promising sounds! In a frantic rush, we dash into the barracks and crouch on the floor. Soon the air erupts with distant thunder. BOOM! BOOM! The earth rumbles. It quivers. Boom! Boom! Are these bombs or flak? Boom! Boom! Please, God, let it be bombs that jolt the earth around us. Shake this earth, allied bombers! Show these Hitlerites how odious you find their treatment of us!

Boom! Boom! Yea! Yea! Drop them right here, right on top of us and our tormentors in one big blast. Crush their enormous city of murder. Boom! Boom! Boom! Yea! Yea! Yea! A thousand times Yea to every one of those Booms! Avenge us brave allies! Unleash your lethal load that'll stop their contemptuous, mocking smirks and replace them with a wide-eyed anguish and paralyzing panic! Let us hear *them* praying to survive! Show *them* they can't murder with impunity!

Soon we hear the menacing drone of aircraft, a sound I first heard five years ago when German planes flew over our defenseless Lodz. It's like the hum of an enormous swarm of drones. There must be dozens of them up there and, as sinister as their rattle sounds, I welcome it as if it were a fanfare, a suspenseful roll of drums before a death-defying circus act. Its ominous whir bodes disaster to our tormentors. What a festive concert! And it intensifies, a joyous rhapsody heralding the impending finale – victory of goodness over evil, an inevitable and crushing retribution. Ah, what harmony of dissonance! Buzz on! Buzz on, you swarm of drones! Bring us deliverance!

Flushed with excitement, I tremble as I crouch on the floor. These primitive barracks offer no defense against bombs. The SS might've just as well left us outside. Surely they're taking cover in shelters. No matter. Let the bombs fall where they may! Let them hit this camp, the SS bunkers and even our barracks! Let us die like our Samson just so we can feel their pain and the scoffs on their smug mugs replaced at last by that jolt of mortal fear. How exhilarating to see *them* scared and running for cover! Even my nagging hunger is gone. My head feels giddy. I'm floating on air. Vengeance, at last!

It's total euphoria. For the first time in these five agonizing years, I can see the beginning of the end. The light at the end of the tunnel. So, the masterful Nazis are *not* as invincible as they made us believe and as they believed themselves to be. At last, they are forced to face the plague that they unleashed on humanity – the horror of a world war. I've lived long enough to see fear on their mugs for the first time. It's a momentous event to witness their vulnerability! Just as Dad's triumphant tale of his witnessing the end of the World War I: how two German officers whined for mercy to their young Polish captors in the streets of Lodz. And it's now about to be repeated.

Poor Dad! Too bad he can't see it again. Will Mom, at least, live to see them lose? Will I?

If I should die now, let me, please, oh Lord, see our assassins as fear replaces their sardonic laughter and indifference to our suffering. Amen! They got us into the barracks surely not for our safety, but to deny us the thrill of seeing fear on their arrogant faces. Maybe my prayer will be more effective if I dust off my Hebrew from five years ago when I prepared for my never-to-be bar-mitzvah. But the words don't come to me.

The booms are fading. The flak and the explosions are more remote. My prayer was for naught. Please return and drop those precious bombs right here. PLEASE!!

My mind drifts to the air-raids that I witnessed in September of 1939. The German bomber formations flew directly overhead, while Lodz was already abandoned by every Polish military unit and lay at the mercy of the advancing Germans. It was a frightful sight: unending tight formations of huge bombers, growling with an awesome deafening roar, suspended ominously low over our beloved city. Our sprawling apartment buildings and textile plants lay helplessly exposed right under the massive underbelly of that brazen monster that hovered over us with impunity. Scared, we waited for the attacker to release his devastating weapons and destroy our peaceful and orderly lives. We were at Aunt Asta's apartment in the center of the city and went down into the cellars to brave the bombs. Some of us received gas-masks, though many didn't think they'd be effective anyway. Others didn't put them on, scoffing that the Germans had their fill of poison gas in World War I, and wouldn't use it fearing retaliation. I put one on but soon took it off because it was so stifling that it didn't even filter out the air in those dank, smelly cellars. Some people braved the air-raids in stairways, but what if the building collapsed?

But the Germans had no need to drop bombs on Lodz, regular or gas ones, for no one bothered to defend it. Lodz was spared from destruction because Hitler regarded her as part of the German Reich Territory, and thus deserved to be preserved in good condition.

No bombs are falling now either. Not nearby. My euphoria is gone. The bursts of flak and thuds of bomb-blasts are growing fainter. The earth is now barely quivering. The air-raid is ending. Maybe they'll strike on their return flight. But my hope dwindles when I realize that they'll have no bombs left. I grow very weary. My despair returns. We've been betrayed, deserted, abandoned. If they dropped only one bomb to put the fear of retribution in the souls of our tormentors, it would maybe curb their wanton mayhem.

The siren blows for the end of the air-raid, and the SS whistles and shouts urge us to return outside. Nothing has changed! Our joy is over. The SS are in charge. Undaunted. Insolent. Arrogant. Self-righteous and self-assured. Now even bolder than before. Their scoffing expressions ooze contempt for us. The pilots spared them and their factory of death.

The allies have worthier objects to worry about than our lives in this death camp. The SS need not fret over their mayhem. The allies won't fuss with them over this place.

Suddenly, I feel a bitter resentment toward the allies, the Russians, the Brits, the French and the Americans. There's no relief in sight for us. Until now, we couldn't even imagine where help would come from. England and the USA were too far away, the Soviets too busy trying to oust the Germans from Russia. And, at last, they showed up. Almost. If they dropped only leaflets in passing over, at least leaflets, stating that they know what goes on in here, then it would give us some hope; that as soon as the smoke clears they'll get even with our tormentors for their evil and hold them responsible for every atrocity. If the SS read them, then they might think twice before tormenting us again.

Now I understand Aunt Hela's first love, Natek, who immigrated to Palestine in 1935 to rebuild the Jewish state. If these planes were sent from a Jewish nation, they'd take drastic action and maybe even drop paratroopers to deliver us from our misery. Hitler wouldn't be able to make Jews stateless if we had our own government to claim us.

I need to share my failed expectations with Lolek and Felek. They're near their barrack and also bitterly disappointed. The bombing objective was the industrial center of Bunau, a rubber plant some distance away. Here, at Auschwitz-Birkenau, we can draw neither joy nor hope from it. Lolek nods in the direction of some SS men: "They know that the allies won't bomb this camp since nothing is produced here but corpses. Now they're even more assured of their own invincibility. They know, they can dispense death, but that retaliation won't touch them. Now more than ever, they're convinced that the war will just pass them by. Just look at their grinning snouts."

The upsurge of hope raised by the sudden air-raid is quashed by my feeling of unrelenting futility. I'm too upset to talk, and I leave the two to mingle with the crowd.

Chapter 24:
A Fresh Resilience

When I later run into the two boys, I share my agitation about the air raid. Lolek, ever the hot-head, bursts out: "If they only dropped a bomb or two we could grab some weapons in the confusion and kill a few SS." Felek, sedate and thoughtful responds with a biblical quote that "a person should strive to be a persecuted one rather than a persecutor." But Lolek flares up: "This just shows how the Jewish religion conditions us to be victims. I'd rather be the victimizer."

"This is no time to think of settling accounts," Felek says. "One has to cling to life as best as one can, for this, in itself, is the only act of defiance for us now. Our victory will come after the war when we re-fashion Poland in the socialist spirit."

Here they are, on the brink of death, still debating on how to better the world.

"Revenge isn't a Jewish tradition," he continues. "We leave retaliation to God. 'Vengeance is mine,' is a privilege reserved only for Him."

But Lolek objects: "Why must we, of all people, be the People of the Book? Why can't we be the People of the Gun? At least, we'd make them fear us. Instead, they only loathe us. Unless they realize that there's a price to pay for Jewish lives, we're all doomed. If we could only let them taste some of their own medicine," he says in a rising voice with his dark eyes flashing menacingly.

"Simmer down, will you," Felek warns. "Someone may report you."

"I don't give a damn," Lolek raises his voice even higher. "Let them denounce me if they feel like it." He's looking fiercely at the inmates around us. "Go ahead, grovel before the Fascist flunkies! Go ahead, toady to the dogs of the bourgeois!"

"That's enough!" hushes Felek. "That talk will get us in trouble. That's all the SS need in here; a Jew who is also a blatant communist. They'll have a ball with you."

"I don't care. Let them kill me as a communist rather than as a Jew. At least I'd feel that I've earned my punishment."

The men around us are now turning around and begin staring at Lolek.

"Let's get out of here!" Felek hisses and hastily pushes Lolek away from the crowd.

Lolek's rebellious spirit is infectious. The very idea of retaliation for all the wrongs inflicted upon us has a resuscitating effect. To die, but not without a worthy cause! Surely not for communism. Why give them credit for my daring? Why can't we raise our own banner and die if necessary, fighting as Jews for our own cause?

Please, Great God, give us a chance to strike back! Provide us with arms, any kind of weapons, even if only like the one that Samson got from the jaw of an ass, to put the fear of the Lord in their vicious hearts. Samson, a national hero who died valiantly dragging his sadistic tormentors with him to death. He should be venerated by us on the same par as Moses. God should give Samson's strength to every abused Jew!

I recall Natek's letter from Palestine to Aunt Hela in which he proudly tells how his pioneer unit resists Arab onslaughts, how it forms small fighting groups who quickly alert each other when their settlements are raided, and how readily they meet them and alert their neighboring settlements. And even though the Brits forbid Jews and Arabs to bear arms, there's no other way to check Arab hostility but to fight back.

My sudden feeling of rebelliousness seems to uplift me as I'm shaking off the self-image of an obedient and cowering victim. My new attitude may show in my behavior, so I quickly merge with the crowd, lest some SS man notices my defiant posture and shoots me on the spot. I am still agog with excitement and think about the bombless air raid.

Chapter 25:
Dreams

onight I dream that Grandpa Saul is chased by jeering German soldiers who beat him with clubs and pull on his beard. I can't bear his humiliation, and, like Moses, I raise the Ten Commandments, which at once turn into the two columns that Samson pushed on the jeering Philistines. "Now you'll pay for this!" I roar, mightily pushing the tablets/columns asunder. They crumble in a mighty blast, engulfing everything in fire and destruction. "You've ruined my world; now see yours vanish!" I yell. A piece of flying debris jolts me in the ribs, and I wake up to the poking of a swearing man, lying nearby. Trying to move away from him, I push myself against a mass of bodies on the floor. The jolt in my ribs is painful, but soon I fall asleep again.

I dream that there's another air-raid with Natek on a rescue mission on one of the planes – good old Natek Praszkier stirred my pride with snapshots from there on which he toiled the land with a rifle on his shoulder. Our inmates yell joyfully over the drone and the burst of flak: "They're here! They're here! Our boys from Palestine came to free us!" I dash out of the barrack and see Natek, just as on his snapshots, tall, tanned, smiling, in a sun helmet and khaki shorts, and with a huge rifle. He's shooting at fleeing SS men who don't even shoot back, but scurry like rats into their air-raid shelters. "Natek, Natek!" I shout, pointing at an SS man running for cover: "There goes one, there, there!" His gun rattles rat-a-tat, rat-a-tat, the flak is bursting, the bombs are exploding, the planes are droning right over our heads, and the conductor, Theodor Ryder, our pre-war neighbor, stands on a podium stretching both arms toward a huge orchestra as the symphony reverberates and the music ascends to Heaven. "*Bitte um Gnade, bitte um Gnade!* (Please have mercy, please have mercy!)" plead the captured SS men with their hands high over their heads. "See, that's how it was," Dad says. "I told you so, see? Look how they tremble! Look! Look how scared they are? Just as in November of 1918."

I nod eagerly: "Yes, yes! Just as you told me, Dad. I see them clearly. Just as you told me, Dad, yes, yes!" I look at Dad, stout and standing next to me, suddenly remembering that he starved to death in the ghetto.

"But aren't you dead, Dad?"

"Yes, I am, but I had to come and see this spectacle again. I wouldn't miss it for anything in the world." I'm so happy for him, I want to hug him, but he vanishes. Instead Natek is next to me, handing me his huge rifle: "Here, now you shoot them a little. I'm going over to see Helenka," (his endearing name for Aunt Hela). I point the rifle at the fleeing SS men, but as I pull the trigger, the barrel droops. I want to return the gun to Natek, but he's gone. The SS men loom larger in size and numbers. They don't run now but stand, watching me attentively, and laugh derisively pointing at my sagging barrel. The inmates run from the bursting bombs and trip and fall on me, hurting me, jabbing me in the neck and in the ribs.

A sharp pain wakes me up. I'm in a tangle of moaning and groaning men, roused to the morning "*Aufstehen!*" As usual, the kapos hop over our bodies, clubbing right and left. Yesterday's air raid hasn't brought us any respite. The end of this war, for us at least, depends solely on the German whim.

Chapter 26:
Doubt in God

We scramble outdoors, rushing into the dark to secure a shielded place inside the "tuft of human grapes". It must be the sixth day in this hell pit. Or is it? I can't keep track of time in here. One day is like another: pain and a daze. Is hell like this? We have no clocks, no calendars, perhaps no future. In the ghetto, we had some sense of time, as we watched an orderly progression of days, weeks, months and years. But here, except for the long wait between feedings, we're unaware of time moving. We're suspended in limbo.

After the morning routine, I find only Felek alone and dejected. The two of them have been inseparable until Lolek was taken away at Appell, probably because of his ravings, Felek frets. We walk silently. But the hunger is tugging and I ask: "Why do the SS treat us like vermin? When they inspected our ghetto workshops, they praised our production and resourcefulness. Here, from their perspective, we've become worthless trash deserving only to be killed."

"Hitler resents us for claiming that God chose us to carry His word," he says, "so he mocks Jewish religious importance by relegating us to an inferior status as a race."

"Yes, but while Hitler does his thing, our Almighty does nothing," I say, waiting for Felek to contradict me and inspire me with some renewed hope in God.

"It's your problem if you still believe in Him, but we must spread a different message to the world. Only universal brotherhood and equality will bring salvation. The rule of the proletariat will prevent the rich and the powerful from amassing all the wealth." All Felek's interpretations of religion lead him to the same conclusion. "Religion is divisive and causes dissent only," he continues. "It fosters discrimination, false pride, elitism. Under communism, there'll be no need to repress those who don't belong to a majority religion because there won't be any. Religion will be rightly relegated to where it belongs: myth, legend, mysticism and superstition. Sensible people will laugh and make fun of it. That special relationship we have with God is wholly one-sided. If God ever had control over the events on Earth, now would be the appropriate time for Him to show it. We're on the brink of extinction, we, who introduced Him to the world as the One and Only at a time when paganism was rife. Shouldn't He do something for us, just out of sheer gratitude? He could easily pull one of His biblical bags of tricks, and smite Hitler with a stroke of lightning, turn him into a pillar of salt, send a flood upon him, or hit him with one of the ten plagues."

"You're blaspheming!"

"So what? If God punishes me for blasphemy and doesn't do anything to the Germans for the murder of our innocents – to hell with Him!"

I shudder. But Felek goes on: "What if Abraham's revelation of the existence of the One and Only God was only wishful thinking? Then the Torah, the New Testament, and the Koran are all based on a myth, on Abraham's singular fantasy. And all the holy scriptures are a sham. And the only Master is man. Man, with his wanton cruelty and his base passions, unrestrained by a higher power, and consistently violating all moral codes; a powerful man to whom others would subject themselves willingly if he just serves their needs and brings them more immediate results and rewards?"

Felek's atheism may work for him. But for me, taking away the hope of a mighty God is unbearable! Because if God is out, then we Jews made a one-sided covenant with a non-existing partner, and our stubborn adherence to piety, devotion, tradition, ethnicity and mosaic morality were all in vain. Especially at this era of our relentless suffering. My faith is hanging on by a thread.

Chapter 27:
Just Another Whack

I'm rambling dizzily toward my barrack. Is it from hunger or from the chaos of Felek's ideas? Surely, he's wrong; probably rebelling against his strict religious upbringing. And he is a Marxist to boot. Anyway, God does exist and will soon… No! *Now*! Smite Hitler, too, and let us celebrate another holiday of survival equal to Passover, Purim or even to Hanukah.

There's a stir nearby: a burly Green Triangle is whacking an inmate who raises his arms to protect his head. He kicks the man in his underbelly. With a painful groan, the man collapses, writhing in convulsions. The effect of the kick pleases the kicker who jauntily says in parting: "*Na, los, schiess im Wind! Damit du noch ein Tag scheissen kannst.* (Get lost now! So that you can go on shitting for one more day.)" The man is on the ground, groaning and twitching. We disperse.

"One more day of shitting," the Green Triangle's words remind me of what we've been reduced to in our abusers' eyes: just a swinish multitude of bedraggled, foul-smelling bodies emitting excrement and concerned only in performing bodily functions.

I drift on. Who will even know if I die here? I'll be as anonymous as every inmate. While Hitler and his top henchmen will forever be assured their place in history books and shrines in their former fortresses and cemeteries, dear Grandpa, Great-grandpa, and my other family patriarchs will be razed from memory forever without a trace of their earthly existence. And there would be no one else who knew them with whom I could share memories. Not even a gravestone or a marker bearing their names! Nothing will be erected anywhere to attest to the fact that they once lived, prospered, led decent and pious lives as devout family men. "May your name and the memory of you be forgotten forever and ever!" is the most damning curse that a Jew can cast on someone, and this is now happening to us. The whole extended families of the Weintraubs, the Riesenbergs, and the Bodzechowskis vel Eichorn, who flourished for centuries, are now reaching their extinction and total oblivion.

Bam! A whack catches me on the right side of my head and sends me reeling, but I keep myself from falling. Quickly, I retrieve my knocked-off cap. The blow stings, but being caught without a cap – a part of one's uniform – is a very serious offense and may be punishable by death. Any SS man can punish me in any way he sees fit for such an infraction of camp regulations. I try to catch a glimpse of the man who whacked me, but all I can see is the stout back of a well-fitting prison uniform disappearing in the crowd. I don't know what I did to earn this whop, but apparently he has enough authority to dispense blows at will when someone's mere presence riles him. But then – what is just another whop on the head in a place such as this, where one's trying hard to evade a clubbing on the skull or a bullet in the head? "Our woes should last only so long as he'll last when I catch him," intoned Moishe Husyd a few days ago, practically involving us all as accomplices in Chief Rozenblat's impending death. But Husyd's invocation didn't cast its magic. Rozenblat is dead, but our affliction is still nowhere near from being over. On the contrary, it seems to intensify.

Chapter 28:
Lolek's Hanging

I catch a glimpse of a familiar face in the crowd. Can it be Lolek? No. And yet, it is! But his face is shriveled and pinched. He got even smaller and appears to be collapsed within himself. It's painful to look at him. This fearless street brawler is now in distress. Even though he still tries to maintain his cocky mien, his walk is strained and he needs the support of Felek, who also looks bad. There are no mirrors in the camp, but it's enough to look at familiar faces to realize how oneself may appear to others. Without seeing the gradual disintegration of known people day after day, it's difficult to recognize those whom one knew just days ago. Would I recognize Mama without her lustrous wavy hair? If I don't see my two acquaintances in a few days, I probably won't even recognize them.

I find out that Lolek was hanged on a pulley for a whole day by his wrists tied behind his back. After a short time, because of his own body weight, his arms were yanked out from their sockets. He suffered dislocations of both his shoulders. He lost consciousness from the unbearable pain, yet they kept him hanging for a long time. Perhaps he'll be more careful next time he feels like spouting off his rebellious ranting and raving. Such phrases as "Fascist flunkies" could have serious consequences here. He's lucky that they didn't kill him altogether. Informers will snitch on fellow prisoners even in here for just another helping of soup. We must beware of eavesdroppers.

We walk in silence slowly. I try to divert Lolek from his agony: "To survive physically, we'll have to survive spiritually." But it rings hollow; just another platitude. Neither of the two even cares to comment. So,

I pose a question: "Do you think that people will believe what they are doing to us in here?"

"If we live long enough to tell them," Felek mutters.

Still trying to distract Lolek, I say: "Maybe the Christians hate us for exerting a moral pressure on mankind, for trying to curb man's evil nature, for our relationship with God?"

But he snaps at me with a surprising energy: "If the godless Soviets don't come soon to liberate us, you'll soon be joining your Lord in Paradise. Only the Red Army will save you so that you can go on raving about your spiritual nonsense. How do you like your Almighty's way of choosing a godless nation as the Soviets to liberate such religious cretins like you? How do you like this for symbolism, my faithful believer?"

His fury stymies my response. I'm glad that his outburst invigorates him and distracts him from pain. He's prodding on: "And what about God's choice for Hitler's birthday, falling right in the middle of Passover, eh? How's that for a cruel joke? Just when Jews prepare to celebrate their delivery from slavery and oppression on this most symbolically significant holiday, God drops another major plague on them – Hitler!"

Lolek is too testy. My attempts to divert him from his pain only flare him up, which is too strenuous for his battered body. Felek is sarcastic. "Look," he says to me in a conciliatory tone: "We've been bamboozled into this faith by our parents and grandparents, but so were they." He explains in detail that our supposedly unique God is an amalgam of various deities from other religions. Felek's breadth of knowledge is impressive but not consoling. I can't give up on my trust in God. Let Felek and Lolek spew their atheism – I'll still keep my faith.

Chapter 29:
Wrong Barrack

T he godlessness of the two boys distresses me. Yet it could be mere posturing. Communists are supposed to be atheists! But what if they are right and we put our trust in a God who's just a figment of mankind's imagination and wishful thinking?

A shrill whistle announces the evening Appell. Hastily I run to my barrack still absorbed in thought. Am I really in a position to forsake God? On the other hand, can I really accept His indifference in this hellhole? Is He really testing us as He did with Job? He surely can see this Murderopolis! How can He not react? Where's a sign of His outrage? To the murder of children? So many children! His children!

I fall in line with the other inmates in front of my barrack. Only it suddenly dawns on me that it is *not* my barrack! I dart out from the already formed rank and dash' toward my barrack. The promenade is empty. All inmates are standing in closed ranks in front of their barracks. I'm the only one racing like a lost soul. I'm frantic. Yesterday, an inmate made the same error and stayed for the count in another barrack. The roll call was delayed for a long time. It wasn't easy to identify him. When they finally found him, they just took his number down. His future doesn't look promising. Maybe he even did it intentionally to be with a relative or a friend. Maybe he tried to get away from an abusive kapo.

Out of breath, I reach my barrack and push myself into the already closed ranks just as the count begins. An alert kapo instantly appears and gives me an awful wallop that sends me reeling, but I try to keep from falling and push myself in between the first two men in the rank. My persistence apparently impresses the kapo because he doesn't hit me again but just warns me that he'll keep an eye on me. Phew! That was close. I must be more alert at every moment.

Chapter 30:
Evoking the Mighty Powers

We're on the floor of our barrack that is again less crowded tonight. I'm trying to stretch out completely for a change. But protruding limbs foil my sleep. Maybe I'll pray. God would be easier to reach if I were in a sanctified place, where He appears in spirit. I recall our grand synagogue on Kosciuszko Boulevard, and the solemn moment when the doors to the ark were about to be opened, and all the men had to cover their heads with prayer shawls to avoid seeing the Spirit of God while we, the boys who couldn't wear them yet before our bar mitzvah, had to shut our eyes and bow our heads. Dad told me that whoever didn't close his eyes at that moment would be struck blind. Now I wonder: If God's Spirit could blind faithful congregation members for such a minor sin, shouldn't It especially punish those who try to destroy His people? If God could only blind *them* even for just an hour, we could make a run from here... If Moses could split the Red Sea just long enough for the Jews to cross it, God could do it again...if..., if..., if...

Oh, Almighty God! How can Thou bear this mayhem? How can Thou not choke on this unstoppable foul smoke rising to Thy Heaven from so many charred human bodies of those on whom Thou bestowed Thy commandments to live righteously?

Intense hunger pangs foil my concentration. I already digested the piece of bread I got as the evening meal, and now my stomach is feeding on my body tissues. I can't sleep. My mind conjures a memory of a seder table with sumptuous Passover dishes. My aunts, uncles and cousins were seated around the elongated and festively bedecked table at Grandpa's apartment, and Grandma kept bringing delicious dishes that she had been preparing for days. I, being the youngest male who could read Hebrew in the Haggadah, asked the Four Questions. I tried to contain my excitement because of the solemnity of the occasion. The adults listened respectfully, admiring my pronunciation of my newly learned Hebrew.

Finally the reading of the Haggadah ended, and everybody started chatting and laughing and indulgingly admonishing us children to behave. By then the ritual four glasses of wine made us giddy, and Stefa and I left our seats and ran around the table thinking up goofy pranks and laughed uproariously for no reason at all. But even Grandpa, who sat solemnly at the head of the table, was indulgent with our silliness. From the kitchen, Grandma ushered in the main dishes in bowls from which delicious, mouth-watering aromas wafted, tantalizing our noses with roasts, fish, chicken soup, macaroons, ah…and what a delightful cacophony of amiable chatter, joyful laughter, and singing of the Haggadah. The daily problems were forgotten for the moment, unpleasant topics were avoided, only mirth reigned to enhance the spirit of that most joyous holiday. One wine glass is set aside for the Prophet Elijah. No, no! Not yet! Let me just dwell a bit longer on the food. Ah, the food! Grandma's dumplings were in the chicken soup. The sizzling cracklings, too. Those luscious, scrumptious, yummy dumplings. I would bite off a chunk and chew, and chew.

And then, finally, the door would be opened slightly so that the invisible Prophet Elijah could enter and take a sip of wine out of the goblet that was set aside for him. Ah, what a sense of awe we experienced then. That glorious feeling that God *is* and that His angels are watching over us, hovering over us and reading our innermost thoughts. And we would banish all unholy thoughts lest they were detected and we were punished for them.

Ah, what a world that was under our elders' supervision, loved and admired by them and by relatives, we grew curious about the universe and its wonders and about the world with its promises of the yet unknown, and trusting that the All-Powerful God had everything under His control, meting out His justice, His rewards, and His punishment.

Sleep is not coming. The jostling of shoes in my face and neck is keeping me awake. Should I pray some more maybe? But Grandpa prayed three times a day, and yet his devotion got him nowhere: he lost his factory – his life's achievement – and was practically banished from most of his beloved children and grandchildren.

Did Hitler rise to power through his prayers? How could God grant a Hitler his wishes? If Hitler resorted to prayer, it must have been to

Satan, and not to God. Only with Satan could a Hitler strike a bargain. The death of so many at the bidding of one man must be the work of an evil force with supernatural powers approaching those of God's. Only Satan could wield such power. And if Hitler indeed derives his evil might by having struck a deal with the devil, then why not put one's trust in the devil and pray to him instead?

What if I summoned Satan and offered to propagate his work of evil on earth, slugging, maiming, and killing indiscriminately man and beast alike? Would he put me up to this task? And would he spare Mama for my loyal servitude? Does Satan spare people, too, or does he only destroy?

Satan, or whatever thy name, I invoke thee! Come forth! Appear before me! Show thyself! But hurry before it's too late! Come and take my soul! I'm offering it to thee for eternal damnation. Thou may burn it forever in the hottest part of hell, but save Mama, Grandpa, my aunts, uncles and my little cousins!

Spare them the agony of *this* hell!

Chapter 31:
A Flicker of Hope

"*Aufstehen! Los, los! Austreten! Rrrraus!* (Up! Fast, fast! Step out! Out!)" The commands reach me as if through a dense fog. Pinned down on the floor by a billowing human mass, I can't rise. Even the instant cracking of clubs against skulls and bones, shrieks, screams, moans and groans seem very remote. But maybe it's safer to stay below this human bulk to avoid direct blows. I've no control in this tumult and resign myself to my doom. Only luck can spare me from getting clubbed; we can't evade blows anymore than soldiers in the line of fire can elude bullets. Except we aren't shooting back, but are on the receiving end only.

Lifted by the human mass, I wind up outside, lucky to have escaped any injury in the scuffle. Again we herd up to escape the morning chill and wait in the dark for the merciful sun to lighten the sky and warm us. The morning chill is more nippy than usual. Even the bodies of the surrounding men can't keep me warm enough. At least in the ghetto we had enough clothing to ward off the cold and could stay indoors and not be outside like cattle. Reminiscing and daydreaming help me to somewhat to escape this gruesome reality. And yet losing awareness of my surroundings bodes disaster as well.

To find some comfort, I search my mind for anything positive or hopeful to think about. Yes! Aunt Hela, the lovely and the youngest of Mama's six sisters, with her energetic husband Sym, had the guts to disregard German orders for this final evacuation. From all my uncles and aunts, only they dared to stay and hide. If the Hitlerites didn't flush them out and kill them, I may still have a living relative when the war is over. That is if I survive myself. If…, a big IF. But a pleasant thought to think about. With this flicker of hope, I may bear the hardships better. If at least they survive, I won't be alone in this world.

Chapter 32: Starving

Again these gnawing hunger pangs tug and tear at my intestines. If I could only, for a minute, sink my teeth into a huge, chunk of bread to chew, and chew, to swallow. Ah, the joy of a full stomach. That wondrous act of filling that gaping, cavernous abyss and end these painful spasms that grind and try to feed on its own lining. The pain stabs at every fiber, every cell in my body. I'm tense, irritable, fidgety, unable to think, to even daydream; it's as if a live animal dwells in my stomach, tearing, gnawing, tugging…preventing me from thinking of anything but food, I can think of nothing but to sate that hunger-dragon, to mollify it, to get it out of me. I can fool the beast by pretending to be chewing, amassing digestive juices in my mouth just as I do during a real feeding so as to appease that creature within that keeps demanding to be fed. I try to stretch the imaginary sop as long as I can until there's nothing to be chewed anymore and only the pap fills my mouth. I swallow and send this fake load down my digestive canal to calm the clawing behemoth below. But the monster nesting in my belly is not fooled. I think the Germans planted it inside me to punish me internally as well as externally. The beast is snapping greedily, ferociously, tugging at my stomach tissues. A series of waves rocks my head with a dull ache at the temples that spreads to the back of my head. If I could only grab something; thrust my hand deep into that cauldron with soup and pull out a potato, shove it down my throat, gulp it down quickly before they could force it out of my mouth, and then…let happen what may. Let them beat me, kick me, I won't care. Just so that I can stifle the pain inside that's pawing and gnawing and tearing. I won't even care if I die under their blows just as the Musulman did.

I must be on the verge of becoming a Musulman myself. Such thoughts are self-defeating. Such recklessness is suicidal. The burly brutes are just lying in wait for a loser whom they would torture with impunity. No! No suicide for me yet. I have to last till noon when I'll be able to still this throbbing stomach with some soup. Maybe I'll even get lucky and find another slice of potato in it. I must withstand these hunger pains. I've had enough practice in these past five years. In the ghetto, at least, we learned quickly how to select plants which could be edible. Marjoram was one of them. But when people discovered that it could be digested, everybody hunted for the elusive plant and even that was soon gone. We also tried laughing because a good belly laugh could fool the stomach into a feeling of fullness. Finding humor even in others' misfortunes would keep some people from losing their minds, even with such pathetic jokes as: "I don't want them to knock on my tombstone, shouting that the war is over." At the time, I tried to sleep off the intense hunger. But it wasn't easy. Such sleep was one continuous, feverish dream of food and eating, which also contained topics of heated conversations with elaborate descriptions of dishes and eating them bite by bite. These talks allayed the hunger only while the images lasted, then it returned harder with a renewed fury.

Even rotten potato peels, discarded by the soup-kitchens, were collected from the ghetto garbage dumps by desperately starving people. These prospectors would take their lucky find home, wash it, boil it, and bake it into a pie. The odious stench gagged us all, but didn't deter these starved human scavengers from eating them. It made us wonder what would come next? What else can a human put in a stomach without being poisoned? For those lucky ones who didn't die from eating this processed garbage, it meant survival for another day – another day that would bring them ever closer to the end of the war.

Chapter 33:
Aunt Hela in Here

T he Appell is over. I'm drifting with the milling inmates. A tall man with a vaguely familiar face stops me: "I'm Monat, the bookkeeper. Your Uncle Sym's friend. Do you remember me?"

I tell him that I do and ask him indifferently how long he's been here. He tells me that he came ten days ago and has been trying to get on a labor gang as a carpenter.

"But it's very risky because they ask you tricky professional questions." I nod.

"Two days ago," he continues, "we tried to get on a work detail with your Uncle Sym, but they rejected me, though he got through and I haven't seen him since."

"UNCLE SYM!" I cry out. "He remained in the ghetto! I left with my mother on the very last train together with Rumkowski. But Uncle Sym and Aunt Hela decided to stay!" I protest vehemently as if my ardent denial could reverse this devastating news.

Mr. Monat gives me a sympathetic look: "Unfortunately there was one more transport after Rumkowski, and Sym and Hela were on it."

I reel back. Aunt Hela *in here*?! No, no! It just can't be! But she and Sym resolved to stay! What could've changed their minds? Surely they were caught, I surmise.

"They were not caught," says Mr. Monat as if reading my mind, but decided to follow the rest of us. "They wanted to share the fate of their loved ones, no matter what."

Dumbfounded, I walk away from him without another word. The oppressive, stifling smoke billows into the silent sky with an intensified strength. My flicker of hope is dead now. Aunt Hela in here?!

Dear, lovely Aunt Hela! Always so close to Mama who derived joy from Hela's beauty and probably guarded her youngest sister from the fate of Aunt Rozia, who had died unwed in the aftermath of an abortion. Both Aunts, Hela and Rozia, doted on me whenever I was dropped off at my grandparents' apartment to have the two babysit with me while Mama went to work at Grandpa's factory. They loved to dance and improvise steps. "Brother, can you spare a dime?" was a popular tango, and Hela and Rozia commiserated with the American worker out on his luck during the Depression. Giving charity was an honored tradition for the Riesenbergs; Hela and Rozia tried to get their friends and acquaintances to send relief packages to America's needy. Hunger or poverty in the USA was just too hard for them to accept.

In those rosy pre-war days, Mama and my aunts fasted briefly on occasions, probably trying to experience hunger as an act of solidarity with those destitute in the world, or maybe because they thought that ample food can't be enjoyed unless one knows the other extreme: intense hunger. It's just like with good health, love, money and freedom – which are cherished more only when one is sorely familiar with the opposite condition. Once, Mama and Aunt Hela came home from shopping so hungry that they claimed to be on the verge of fainting. They brought a loaf of fragrant fresh pumpernickel filled with raisins. They salivated in anticipation of eating that delicious bread. Maybe it was all part of warding off the "evil eye", as if they were saying, "Here, we fasted and are now about to enjoy a simple slice of black bread with butter," while in reality the family enjoyed opulence. Perhaps this was their way of easing their guilt in a world rampant with suffering and destitution. Apparently, all this posturing didn't fool the "evil eye", which eventually caused their families to suffer real starvation as well as the loss of all their earthly possessions. Ah! That freshly baked pumpernickel, tasty, studded with those delicious raisins!

And now both are here – Mama and Hela. Will they find each other in the women's camp among these thousands of women? Will they recognize each other without their luscious hair? It would be easier for them together. They could console each other. They must keep their hope up. They mustn't die. But what if they don't meet? Mama still thinks that Aunt Hela is in the ghetto. So would I have if I hadn't run into Uncle Sym's friend.

Chapter 34:
A Failed Test

"**M**asons and electricians, assemble for work detail!"

I snap out of my day-dreaming. I've lost awareness of reality and don't even know the time of day. But the call for work electrifies me. *Electricians*! That's *me*!! Here's a chance for *me* to leave this Murderopolis! The caller is the same Work-Kapo Tadek, a squat, square-shouldered Pole who had recruited carpenters and masons a few days ago.

"We need electricians and masons to go on a work detail to another nearby camp!" he loudly repeats his rallying call now in Polish.

My recent apathy and resignation give way to a sudden burst of energy. "Yes, that's me!" I shout back in Polish, drawing myself up.

"You an electrician?" The kapo stops and regards me disdainfully. I cringe under his incredulous glare. My sudden exhilaration gives way to an instant despair. I nod.

"Then tell me, what does a light bulb consist of?" he commands in such a tone as if one has to be a great scientist to know the answer to this simple question.

His peremptory tone and the trivial question stump me, but noticing the impatient and hostile glances of the hefty flunkies accompanying him, I quickly try to collect my thoughts – a glass container, a vacuum, a tiny metal wire made of tungsten – that must be it. There is nothing else that I can think of. And before I can even utter my answer, the briskly stepping Kapo Tadek, probably regarding my hesitation as a failure to pass his arcane little test, is already on his way with his entourage to interview the next candidate who's already pushing himself in and jostling me away.

I'm crestfallen. My momentary rush ebbs. I missed my chance to exit from this morass of death. Who'd expect such a trivial question like that? If they need electricians, it's most likely for installations of new power lines or to repair existing ones. Why ask about the make-up of a light bulb? But that's probably the only thing about electricity that this squat Work-Kapo knows, and he flaunts it in making his selections.

Now what? I've lost my chance to do something for which I was trained. If I get on some work crew now, it'll most likely be for some physical and unskilled labor like carrying rocks or something. But with specialized skills, we may be treated better.

I must get out of this hell-hole soon, very soon. It's too dangerous to remain here where every waking hour is a struggle to outlast starvation and evade a debilitating whacking.

I seek out my two talk-mates to share this failed opportunity. Maybe they, too, heard the work-kapo, applied for the crew and were accepted. I have trouble finding them. Maybe they already left the camp with a work crew. Finally I find them. Yes, they applied; he tested them and accepted them. He asked them the same question, which they answered promptly and correctly. Kapo Tadek's flunkies wrote down Lolek's and Felek's numbers, and tomorrow at *Appel*, they'll join a work crew out of here. I'm glad for them, yet angry with myself for my slack response. Without the two to talk with and get my mind off the hunger, it'll be much harder to pass time. I need to connect with others to also lessen Mama's absence weighing on my mind. If I only hadn't stammered to Kapo Tadek, he'd have accepted me, too, and the three of us would be working together. Now we are meeting for the last time.

Chapter 35:
Out Through the Chimney

A nother gruesome rousing call occurs hours before dawn. I jump up quickly to evade the clubbing and rush outside to secure my place in the midst of the herd where I resume sleeping. Every man is absorbed with gloomy thoughts of wives and daughters, most of whom were surely killed on arrival, filling us all with hopelessness and apathy.

It must be a week that I've been here already. The "welcoming" kapos warned us that "the strongest among you won't last more than two to three weeks at the most," but I doubt that I'll even last that second week. And if I die afar from my two uncles, my death will be anonymous, just another statistic reported at Appell, just a number added routinely to the sea of nameless men whose lives are snuffed out daily for no reason at all. Dying must be easier when you're amidst loving and caring people who'll miss you and fondly remember you…maybe even visit your grave. At least Dad has a grave that I can visit. If I survive, that is. But where would I look for Mama's? Or of all my other relatives?

Death doesn't even shock us in here because it will release us from this agony; it is that final moment when emotions lapse into unconsciousness. The physical pain becomes so unbearable that the mind switches off and gives up trying to control the senses and withdraws into a blissful oblivion of all earthly matters, especially pain, and frees us from our temporal mantle. It may not even be so dreadful were it not for its irreversible finality; I shudder at my thoughts. This is not the way for a seventeen-year-old to think.

"There's no way out of here except through the chimney," the kapos taunted us on arrival, "and then you will meet your Maker." Why would our Maker accept little children before they even had a chance to praise Him in gratitude for His act of their creation? But one doesn't question God.

"God knows what He is doing," Dad used to say, thus closing any further discussion on injustice or suffering. "If we knew what God is doing, and what His plans are for the future of this world, we'd be like Him, and no human being can be like God," he would conclude. But isn't it presumptuous of us to state with such certainty what God knows or doesn't know? Doesn't it imply that we, in fact, do evaluate His actions to be purposeful?

Chapter 36:
One Morning Drill

It's dawning at last. Time for morning Appell. While we stand in ranks waiting for the SS officer to come and take the count, the kapos put us through strenuous drills they call "sport" or "exercise" as if that's what our lazy, overfed bodies need to stay healthy. The hardest are knee-bends; with our arms stretched forwards, we must rise on our toes and very slowly lower ourselves down into a squatting position. This drill is really a torture in the guise of an exercise. We try to reduce the strain by rising and squatting faster when the kapos aren't looking at us directly. For older men, the strain is even greater because their leg muscles are less flexible and the effort causes them to totter and fall. The predatory kapos are just waiting for this and pummel these men with fists and clubs. If they dislike any particular inmate, they can vent their sadistic urges and drill him some more until he drops from exhaustion. Cheating is risky because the kapos take such evasions of their "exercise" personally. But for us, the ones carrying out this grueling drill, it can have fatal consequences as well.

"*Knie-beugen! Eins, zwei, drei, vier* (Knee bending! One, two, three, four)." The drill kapo's count indicates the tempo of either raising or lowering ourselves. On the third slow sit-down, I feel that my leg muscles are too strained for the slow rise, and I rise quickly instead. But my evasive move doesn't escape one kapo's attention. He's next to me in a flash, his massive bulk towering and leaning over me, practically tipping me over as he bellows his command right into my ear: "*Knie-beugen! Eins, zwei, drei, vier.*" His count is even slower now. He's a sturdy brute with the neck of a bulldog. I strain myself to prolong the duration of my "exercise". My knees shake from the strain while I'm trembling from fear of punishment.

But instantly, the kapo's attention is diverted to another inmate. He leaps over to him and whacks him across the face. "Cheating, eh? You thought I didn't see you, eh?" He whacks him again. The man collapses. The kapo orders two nearby inmates to prop him up. "*Knie-beugen!*" he roars into his ear as the man is propped up. The man, about fifty, tries to squat slower but totters and falls again. The kapo raises his foot to kick him, but another inmate darts out to aid the fallen man and saves him from the kapo's boot. He may be a relative or a good friend. "So that's how it is?!" the kapo roars in his accented German. "We have a little goodie-goodie helper here, don't we?" The younger man answers quietly, which I can't make out, but it enrages the kapo. "*Ty shpatna potvora* (You ugly monster)!" the kapo bellows in his apparently native Slovak, or maybe Czech, and follows this with a rapid string of curses. He calls out for assistance to another kapo, a tall, muscle-bound bully with powerful gorilla-like arms, and tells him to grab a hold of the Good Samaritan.

"I'll teach you not to interfere with punishment," he yells in his broken German. "You want to be good to others, you sack of shit? Here you can only be good to yourself."

Together, with all their might, they slam the two inmates against each other's backs. A loud crack is heard as the two skulls collide. The two collapse. Both kapos jump on them and bounce on them, kicking them in the ribs, on the heads, in their faces. The older man soon stops showing any sign of life. The younger one keeps raising his hands to protect his profusely bleeding face and head. Spitting out teeth and blood as the kapo punches his face, he's pleading: "*Warum? Warum?* (Why? Why?)" At last he, too, collapses. I quiver as I look at him, thinking that just moments ago I could have been in his place. And I suddenly realize that I'm still not out of danger once the kapo finishes with him.

"Punishment is given to those who break camp regulation," grunts the Slovak kapo out of breath. "If you help someone who's being punished, you, too, will be punished," he announces with an affected importance. He is panting. "What are you gaping at?" he roars at an inmate nearby. "Do you want some, too?"

I quickly look away from the two battered bodies now on the ground, one showing no signs of life, the other bloodied and slowly twitching. I draw myself up to attention. I look straight ahead, but am wary of the two kapos. Their clubs could crush me if they gang up on me. The first kapo may still come over to finish with me. These brutes stifle any camaraderie among prisoners. The 'ka' in kapo stands for "kameraden" (comrades), which is just another ironic twist in the German camp vocabulary; these thugs are no one's comrades. To them and to the SS we are just scum, a subhuman species, unworthy of such noble Nazi-Supermen gestures as camaraderie.

"*Achtung!*" A shrill whistle announces the arrival of an SS officer to check the count of the morning roll-call. The drill is over. My knees are visibly shaking and my leg muscles feel like cotton. I wish the Appell could continue longer so that the Slovak kapo would forget that he had an issue with me. The SS officer takes the count of us who are standing and of the several bodies stretched out on the ground, some of which were dragged out from the barrack after the reveille or beaten unconscious right here during the drill. Some are still twitching, some are showing occasional signs of life as their chests keep heaving. But the SS officer pays no attention to them, and after accepting the count, he briskly strides off indifferent to the kapos' abuse of us.

Chapter 37:
The Mothers

My knees are still shaking as I totter to the latrine. The deadly beatings that I just witnessed are still before my eyes. And I thought I'd gotten used to this mayhem already. Maybe I was too closely involved this time.

Does the women's camp have to go through these "exercises"? Do the kapos taunt them, too, saying that they have only two weeks to live and that their dearest ones are up the "Heavenly Road" on their way to a "Jew Heaven" as they point to the non-stop smoke billowing up to the sky? Such cruel gibes about a woman's beloved daughters, sisters and nieces may drive them mad. Surely Aunts Asta and Andzia would not part from their little ones and would go with them to share their fate even if they assumed the worst. Separating parents from their little children must be the cruelest of crimes.

Our Jewish national tragedy is symbolized by the Wailing Wall in Jerusalem to remind us of the destruction of our Temple and our subsequent dispersion to the diaspora. But we have a new symbol of our national tragedy, now with a more personal, human aspect: a mother holding onto her child as it is being torn from her by a German soldier.

The altruistic Jewish mother sacrifices herself for her children while we, the children, accept this as natural, unaware of what these devoted, saintly women go through to save us from even a slight discomfort. Carefree and self-centered, we never give it a thought that they won't be here forever and that we may lose them sooner than we think. And they try protecting us from life's shadier sides by not letting us in on what troubles them.

Mama was always upbeat. Even on her menial job at the Carpet Weaving Plant or at the Straw Boots Assembling Plant that made straw boots for German soldiers where I once visited her, she joked, sang and even cheered up her women co-workers. Even after she had been summoned to the much-dreaded Kripo (Criminal Police – a branch of Gestapo) in the ghetto, where they tortured Jews to reveal their hidden valuables, she returned, smiling and reassuring, as if staying together was the natural course of things for us.

We've been here a week maybe. Is Mama still alive? Have they recruited her for outside work yet? Could she have died already without my sensing it? Will I ever find out? Who'll tell me? If her death will be as anonymous as everyone else's, I'll never find out. Would she signal her death to me in some supernatural way?

Is she alone or has she met someone she knows? I can't think of her in these de-humanizing zebra-stripes as still hale, hearty and cheerful. She's probably worried sick over me right now. She's probably saving her pitiful piece of daily bread ration to somehow deliver it to me. Even now, in this hellhole, separated by rows of high-powered wires and with sentries up on their towers guarding so that no one gets even near those wires, she's probably trying to get near them to talk to someone in the men's camp and to summon me so that she could throw her bread – her life – to me.

What a topsy-turvy world this has become; at one time, this special relationship between mothers and their children was honored, and they were always given priority in rescuing attempts during disasters. But in today's world of German domination, mothers and their children are first to be marked for… No! My mind still refuses to grasp it!

An evil Pharaoh once singled out Jewish children, first-born males, for slaughter. But those were biblical times, rife with barbarity and superstition. And, fortunately, we had our Almighty God then, ever so ready and willing to actively intercede on our behalf just in the nick of time.

Now, not He, nor even our mothers, can save us.

Chapter 38:
On My Way Out

I s it before noon or after? The day is gray, dreary, overcast. My hunger is agonizing so it must be near feeding time, either the midday soup or the evening slice of bread.

Is Mama still optimistic, cheerful and professing her "cast bread at your enemies instead of stones"? Would Dad still claim his ever reassuring, "God knows what He is doing," when all the goings-on here are screaming for retribution? And where, *at last* is our Almighty, who in biblical times always punished those bent on destroying us?

"*Electricians*! We need electricians!" There's a stir. I'm back to reality and I, too, jostle through the quivering mob to get closer. Here again is the Work-Kapo Tadek, recruiting masons, cabinet-makers, and: "We need electricians," he shouts in Polish, loud and clear. *Electricians*! Here is my second chance to get out of here! I force my way through the mob and approach him boldly, hoping that he wouldn't remember me from my previous failure. He doesn't. Sure enough he poses the same question: "What are the components of an electric bulb?" Only this time I am ready: "They consist of glass, a vacuum, and a Wolfram or Tungsten filament," I rattle off smoothly in Polish.

He is impressed: "Step out over here! You'll be going to work tomorrow morning."

I'm elated as he tells his aide to take my number and orders me to report to Barrack 26 for the evening Appell. My life's has just been extended; I feel the relief of one condemned to die when a stay of execution is delivered at the last moment. If Mama only knew that I've been selected for work – and as an electrician, no less. A skilled professional and I'm only seventeen. She would be so proud of me. And Dad, too. And Grandpa. Although his hopes for me were more in advanced schooling rather than in crafts. But the Nazis have no use for Jewish intellectuals. They need skilled workers and technicians. And they found a use for me with my technical knowledge. My training in the Electro-technical Workshop provided me with a survival skill. That's something to be thankful for. Now I have a chance to live a bit longer. Maybe long enough to reach our longed-for liberation.

Tomorrow I'll be out of here, away from this Murderopolis where slaughter is so rampant that it's routine – away from this noxious smoke – of human flesh, most likely. I'll leave for a work-camp where there'll be more food, and no random killing – not even beatings.

I'm excited; I can't wait for the day to pass fast enough. I haven't even eaten my slice of bread yet since it was doled out as the evening ration. I'm saving it in my pocket thinking that tomorrow I may have enough to eat and I could give this slice to Mama. But how can I get it to her?

I duly report to my newly assigned Barrack 26 for the evening Appell. This barrack is much emptier, and I stretch out on the floor, which I couldn't do for a week. But my excitement keeps me awake, as does my stomach that growls like an angry animal clamoring for his due. At last my feverish thoughts succumb to an overwhelming fatigue and I drift off to sleep.

I dream that I stroll on the streets of Lodz, enter Grandpa's flat at 26 Piotrkowska Street, sit down at the dining-room table to play checkers with him and nibble on hot chick peas. Stroking his beard, he's mulling over his next move. Then Dad enters, admonishing me about doing homework and that, as punishment, he'll put me in the public school with riff-raff kids. Next I am graduating and all congratulate me as I stand with the diploma in my hand. Then I am under the canopy at my wedding and get off the podium to hug my children. And I present it all to Mama and Dad – the diploma, my bride and the children – and Mama is deliriously happy as she hugs and kisses the little tots, and Grandpa is standing in the background in his dark hat and dark glasses noding with approval. And I'm so happy, so happy. Life is turning out so beautiful, sooo beautiful.

"*Aufstehen, aufstehen! Los, los! Aufstehen!*" The kapos' rousing calls are like a whiplash. In an instant, I'm on my feet trying to evade their wrecking blows. But there's no clubbing in this barrack, not on the selected craftsmen that we've now become.

After the Appell we line up for the tattooing administered by two prisoner orderlies. One of them firmly holds my left arm while the other pricks the inside of my forearm with a tattooing device. After a couple of minutes I'm branded with a capital B followed by 10001. The amused tattoo-expert points out to the other orderly the unusual symmetry of it. My new identification differs from the number sewn on my jacket. Like branded cattle, I'm now the official property of the Third Reich. Any attempt to escape from my German masters will henceforth be frustrated by this permanent seal on my body.

But rather than feeling upset for being branded like cattle, I'm proud of my tattoo. It is a mark of distinction as a qualified worker assured to be left alive! Glad to be leaving this pit of death, I'm also heartsick to leave Mama behind even though we've had no contact between us; we may as well be miles apart. Maybe I could somehow let her know of my good luck, or maybe send her my bread ration. But how? Even if I yell to some woman standing near those wires, and even if she agrees to take the bread and the message, how do I know that she'd deliver them and not eat the bread herself? There must be a thousand men in my barrack alone. And there must be at least twenty-five to thirty barracks in men's camp. I don't even know one inmate in my barrack, nor any of those who prop me up as we stand in the pre-dawn every morning.

Absentmindedly, I walk toward the wires that separate the women's camp from ours. My last evening bread ration is still in my pocket burning a hole in it because I'm starved and am barely restraining myself from devouring it in two gulps. I drift toward the deadly wires. There are no inmates lingering here. It's a danger zone. Posters of a skull and crossbones are displayed all around, practically screaming their warnings of danger. I hesitate. Why am I doing this? Maybe by some miracle Mama will show up on the other side and wave to me. But how will I know her from so far away, in stripes and without her chestnut locks. I still visualize her in her pre-war finery, a stylish wide-brimmed hat, a silver fox wrapped over her shoulders, and her big, beautiful blue eyes beaming at me with pride and joy – and that lovely fragrance of gardenias wafting about her.

I'm sharing my good fate with a kind-faced man that I'm on my way out of here as an electrician. He sighs: "It's just another deception. You'll be sent to a nearby coal mine or a rubber plant if you're lucky; there, at least, you won't have to work outside and freeze."

"A coal mine?!" I echo incredulously.

"Yes. There are lots of them in the neighboring Silesia, and they need hands to load coal. It's an exhaustive labor in soggy soil and dangerous caves saturated with noxious gasses. And the soup isn't that much more nourishing than here."

"A coal mine…," I repeat blankly.

"I went to work out of here as a brick layer," he says. "But there was no construction work. The Germans are only destroying everything and looting the country. I wound up carrying rocks outdoors and it nearly killed me. This is just one of their little deceptions with which they amuse themselves. They select professionals only to send us to all kinds of menial physical labor. You're better off staying here where, at least, you don't have to work so that you can preserve what strength you have left. Out there you won't last as long. *'Arbeit macht frei'* really means that their work will set you free of your very life."

My elation is gone. Doubt sinks in. How can anyone prefer this vast death-house to anything beyond it? But I've no choice now. They got my number. Maybe the man was just envious that I'm on my way out. Maybe he just fell in with a rough work crew. Yet, he may be right; I recall the inmates who worked with wheelbarrows when my cattle-train was pulling into the depot and how the squat SS officer tossed a rock at them.

But what if I heed his warning and don't show up for work when they call out my number? They can make a big fuss and search for me and maybe punish me. Or maybe they will just forget about me and leave me here to my certain death, which could come in another few days as my "two to three weeks" of life in here expires. Or maybe death will come even sooner if my luck at evading the morning clubbing runs out.

Chapter 39:
The Ashes of Auschwitz

Maybe I shouldn't have shared my "good" news. My lucky selection for a specialized profession may be, as the man said, just another SS deception meant to disappoint at the moment of my joy; when I report for work as an electrician, maybe they'll order me to load coals instead. The insidious Nazis like to keep us confused. We never know which decision to make. Mama used to decide for the two of us. Now I'm on my own. What to do?

I must get away from this suffocating smoke and the murderous kapos even if I do wind up in a coal mine or rubber plant. These noxious fumes of burnt flesh have permeated every pore of my body and ingrained themselves in me to the point that I'll probably never be able to be rid of them. In ancient Jewish custom, mourners covered themselves with ashes for only one week, the duration of their bereavement, but these ashes, the Ashes of Auschwitz, will probably stick to me forever like my own skin. And they are most certainly all that is left of my dearest ones who have no resting place for their remains except in my fading memory. So long as I remain alive, they will, too, in the sanctuary of my mind. These ashes will forever cast a shadow over any joy that I may find in the normal world – should such a world ever again be possible for me. They'll always remind me that mankind's capacity for wanton destruction has never abated despite twenty centuries of humanistic progress and the alleged triumphs of Western culture over the dark forces of ignorance, backwardness and superstition. Europe's earlier barbarities and persecutions such as the plunder and mayhem of the Crusaders, the confinement of Jews in Italian ghettoes, the Inquisition, the witch burnings and the pogroms in Eastern Europe all pale before this monstrosity here, where thousands, maybe millions, are shipped in box cars and, by ever deceptive means, disposed of like vermin.

"See the smoke?" the kapos mocked us on our arrival. "That's your parents on their way to Heaven." But what if there really is a Heaven? What if at least some of us will gain admittance to that coveted hereafter? Grandpa Saul could surely claim this privilege. Loved by his family and employees alike, he was kind and never harmed anyone. Will he, for all his piety and goodness, be granted his place in God's presence or will he, like I, prefer Paradise to be a reunion with his mother and father? Only then, as a child, under the watchful eyes of my parents, did I feel safe, secure and immortal with a blissful illusion that all was well and that the world was ideal. That is the true Eden! Perhaps that's why the most severe punishment inflicted on mankind in the Bible is Adam's and Eve's banishment from Paradise, their home, far from their Maker's safe Heaven – just as I'll be from now on.

A dreadful vision from long ago returns to haunt me, a thought I had at five or maybe at six years, a pampered child's worst nightmare – only it's not a nightmare anymore. Now it is real. I'm alone, abandoned. My parents, grandparents, aunts, uncles and cousins are all gone. There's a frightful emptiness all around me; a silent, scary void.

I'm near the deadly wires. A haunting melody of a Viennese waltz is rebounding from somewhere. It must be the camp orchestra, a heavenly music in a hell like this is so utterly incongruous in here, that it is surely another Nazi attempt at humor, this joyous, carefree waltz.

I visualize a memory of a spinning couple dancing in total abandon. The woman's head is thrown back, her arms widely arched, her partner's arm gracefully under her shoulder blades. Whirling, I envision myself in my crib gripping the rail with my tiny hands. My eyes follow the couples swirling in our living room to the tunes of dance music. My parents are celebrating something and everybody is elated. Dad calls out directions, and the couples break into a group dance with all of them facing each other in two rows. Always sensitive to music, I'm jumping up and down in delight while holding on to the crib rail. The music is exciting enough even without the couples floating in rapture. Suddenly, my vision takes a ghastly turn; the floor is filled to capacity with naked, writhing bodies interlocked and climbing over each other, barfing and befouling each other, eyes popping out of their sockets, blood bursting out of noses and ears, faces contorted in extreme agony...

Grotesque images keep fleeting through my feverish mind as I grasp the piece of bread I've been saving for Mama and move forward as if against my will, again, toward the wires that separate us from the women's camp. I'm now close enough to recognize individual silhouettes, but am still unable to tell if these are the figures of women. It's hard to tell from this distance if these ghostly apparitions in baggy stripes without a trace of limber roundness or mellowing softness are really women.

I need to get nearer; the soil is cloddy here; I keep tripping...

...I'm inching closer to the high-tension wires..., maybe too close...

...The sentry stirs in his tower, readying his gun...

...I stumble...

...There is a flash, a whiz...

...My arms are flapping for balance...

...I fall to the ground as gunshots ring out...

...My hand is up in the air grasping the bread...

...It mustn't get dirty...; the soil is sludgy...

...Mama! Mama! I want to shout..., or maybe I am...

...Mommy, please, take this bread from me. It's burning in my hand...

...Take it now, please..., for tomorrow may never come...

...I try to rise, but keep slipping and falling back in the muck...

...I ache...; it hurts...

...The bread must be all dirty now...

...Please, take it, Mama...

Photos

Szymon Weintraub (author's father)

Dora Weintraub nee Riesenberg
(author's mother)

Asta Wolborski (author's aunt) with Henryk Wolborski (husband of Aunt Asta)

Stefa Wolborski (author's cousin) with her mother Asta Wolborski (author's aunt)

Lilka & Stefa Wolborski (author's first cousins); 1935

Asta Wolborski (author's aunt) with daughter Stefa (author's cousin) in Lodz; 1939

Rysia Lawit (author's first cousin); 1935

Rysia Lawit (author's second cousin) standing second from the left in a shelter for children in ghetto.

Katzenelson Academy elementary school graduating class of 1939. The author is standing up at the extreme left in top row.

Katzenelson Summer Cottage in Wlodzimierzow. (Itzhak Katzenelson and his younger brother on first photo)

Chaim Rumkowski, (in glasses) the Eldest of the Jews in the Lodz Ghetto and his Chief of Ghetto Police Leon Rozenblat

Julek and Benek Maliniak (author's second cousins) with mother Rozia; 1939

Aunt Rozia Riesenberg
(author's mother's second youngest sister).

Ala Brzezinska whom Uncle David
married in 1938

David Riesenberg (author's mother's
youngest brother) with Hela Brodt.

Riesenberg and Bodzechowski families. Family photograph taken in late October of 1926 (twenty-eight members, one of which is the author's mother about to give birth to him. She is sitting at the extreme right in an inverted chair to camouflage her advanced pregnancy. Her husband Szymon Weintraub is standing behind her. Her grandfather Szlomo Meyer Bodzechowski vel Eichorn is the second sitting next to her; her mother Tamara Riesenberg nee Bodzechowski vel Eichorn is the sixth one sitting next to her and her father Szaul Avner Riesenberg is standing behind Tamara second from the left. top row.

Author's ghetto ID (front) with his photo on it in 1942

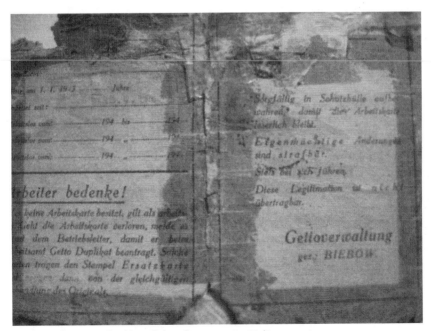

Author's ghetto ID (back) with his photo on it in 1942

Epilogue

I survived Auschwitz, although my spirit was killed there. My selection as an electrician was a deception as I and the other chosen craftsmen wound up loading coal onto lorries in a coal mine not far from Auschwitz. This camp was fortunately not a death-camp like Auschwitz. However, there was a selection in the infirmary where I was laid out with a severe case of the flu right after my first nightshift job in the mine. The SS doctor came from Auschwitz and shipped approximately forty patients to the Auschwitz gas chambers. The doctor who was in charge of this infirmary was a Hungarian Jew named Dr. Kovacs. Even though I was delirious and with a high fever, I remember him interceding on my behalf with the SS doctor from Auschwitz who was checking out my buttocks to make sure that I had enough flesh to let me survive another day: "This boy has only the flu, but will be all right in a couple of days to resume his work in the mine."

In this camp a Christmas/New Year show was staged by some inmates for the SS during the last week of 1944 (inmates were admitted too); a display of creative genius of men in the most dire of circumstances; a costumed farce of a musical tour around the world with dances, songs and humor. Sitting in the audience, I was encouraged by the appreciative peals of laughter of our SS lords in the front row. I thought that there might be some hope for humanity if only to enjoy together a civilized cultural entertainment untrammeled by hatred-fomenting political, racial or religious shamans. (The director and choreographer of this ingenious review was Zev Danziger who survived the war and whom I saw later in Bergen Belsen.)

As the Red Army advanced, Auschwitz, along with all adjoining camps, was evacuated in January 1945, and thousands of inmates were marched off west and away from the front. Thousands died or were shot on the way. After a few days of this murderous march in deep snow, I, and a fellow inmate, Oscar Levin from Luxembourg, escaped at night trying to make our way toward the oncoming Russians. After a few days of freedom, we were caught, jailed, and shipped off to Mauthausen – another concentration camp in Austria, not far from where we were liberated by the American Army in May 1945.

As soon as my health improved somewhat, I returned to Lodz in search of my many relatives, but in vain. Remaining in my native city, where familiar sights kept reminding me of those who didn't return and of my lost childhood, became intolerable.

I soon returned to Germany to a Displaced Person's Camp from which I immigrated to the USA in 1948. I never gave up my search for surviving relatives and recovered two second cousins, brothers Julek and Bernard Maliniak, who had survived only because they managed to escape to the Soviet Union just before the Germans conquered Lodz. It seems that my friend Lolek's observation was indeed realized: the "Godless Soviets" did save my cousins, while the entire Christian world remained passive and uncaring. From my two cousins I got an address of a grand-uncle, Joel Davis, who immigrated to the USA in 1899. When he visited Lodz in 1926, most of our family assembled for a group photo. Thanks to that visit, I was able to see, again, after twenty years, Mama, Dad and all my dear relatives – if only on a photo.

Appendix

Bodzechowski vel Eichorn, Szlomo Mayer – Maternal great-grandfather, b. circa 1860. Last heard of in 1940 in Lodz.

Bodzechowski, Baruch – A distant cousin of Szlomo Mayer to whose daughter, Dora, he was married. Last seen in the Lodz Ghetto in 1944.

Bodzechowska, Dora – Baruch's wife and my great-aunt. Last seen in 1944.

Bodzechowski, Jakub (Jerzyk) – Engineer. Dora's and Baruch's son, b. circa 1915. Shot with his wife and two little children in the Czestochowa Ghetto where he was a policeman.

Bodzechowska, Rozia – Jakub's sister. In the Lodz-Ghetto with her little son till 1944.

Bodzechowska, Fela – Rozia's sister, b. circa 1917. Married to a Maliniak with whom she had two little children. All four perished after the ghetto in Czestochowa was liquidated.

Brodt, Lonia nee Wolborski – A sister of Uncle Heniek Wolborski, b. circa 1898. Survived in Warsaw on "Aryan Papers" with her infant grandson, Izio Kohn. Died in 1977 in Israel.

Brodt, Hela – Lonia's daughter, b. circa 1917. Died in Auschwitz as a Polish woman.

Brodt, Semek – Hela's brother, b.1925. Survived Auschwitz as a Pole. Died 1984 in Berlin.

Brzezinska, Ala – Married Uncle David Riesenberg in 1938, b. circa 1916. Probably killed in Treblinka.

Davis, Joel – b. in 1886 as Bodzechowski, the only son of Szlomo Mayer. Imigrated to the USA in the beginning of the 20th century. Died in 1971 in Florida.

Lawit, Andzia, nee Riesenberg – Mama's younger sister, b. circa 1912. Last seen in the Lodz Ghetto in 1944.

Lawit, Ignatz – Andzia's husband. Last seen in Auschwitz in the first week of September 1944.

Lawit, Gizia – b. 1932, Andzia's and Ignatz' older daughter. Last seen 1944 in the ghetto.

Lawit, Rysia – b.1934. Andzia's and Ignatz' younger daughter. Last seen 1944 in the ghetto.

Lenga, Edzia – (see: Riesenberg, Herman)

Maliniak, Rozia nee Bodzechowska – My great-aunt. Died in the Lodz-Ghetto in 1943.

Maliniak, Aaron – Rozia's husband, escaped from the Lodz-Ghetto in 1940 for the third time, but never heard from again.

Maliniak, Julek – Son of Rozia and Aaron, b. 1919 in Lodz. Survived in the USSR. Died in 1987.

Maliniak Bernard – Julek's brother, b.1921. Survived the war in the USSR. Died in Israel in 1984.

Opatowska, Renia nee Riesenberg – Mama's younger sister, b. circa 1901. Last seen in 1940 in the ghetto.

Opatowski, Sewek – Aunt Renia's husband. Died in Warsaw in 1939.

Opatowska, Mirka – b. 1933. Renia's and Sewek's only daughter. Last seen in 1940 in Lodz.

Riesenberg, Szaul-Avner – Mama's father, b.1875 in Czajkowice near Staszow in Poland. Left Lodz in 1939 for his native shtetl. Killed in Treblinka around 1942.

Riesenberg, Herman – Szaul's older son, Mama's brother. Last seen in Lodz in 1939.

Riesenberg, Edzia nee Lenga – Herman's wife. Last seen in Lodz in 1939.

Riesenberg, Zdzisio – b. 1934 in Lodz. Herman's and Edzia's older son.

Riesenberg, Rysio – b.1935 in Lodz. Herman's and Edzia's younger son.

Riesenberg, David – Szaul's younger son. Left Lodz with his father and his wife in 1939.

Riesenberg, Ala nee Brzezinska – David's wife. Left Lodz with David in September 1939.

Weintraub nee Riesenberg, Dora – My Mother, Szaul's eldest child b.1897. Selected for work in Auschwitz on 8/31/44.

Weintraub, Szymon – b.1890, my father and Dora's husband. Starved in the Lodz Ghetto on April 7, 1941.

Weintraub, Lola – My cousin, b. circa 1919 in Lodz. Last seen in 1939 in Lodz.

Weintraub, Nachman – Lola's father. Starved to death in the Lodz Ghetto in 1941.

Weintraub, Pesa – Lola's mother and my father's sister. Last seen in the Lodz Ghetto in 1943.

Wester, Hela nee Riesenberg – Mama's youngest sister, b.1916. Last seen in August 1944.

Wester, Sym – Hela's husband. Sent to Gross-Rosen Concentration Camp in 1944.

Wolborska, Asta nee Riesenberg – Mama's younger sister. In the Lodz-Ghetto until 1944.

Wolborski, Heniek – Husband of Asta, Mama's younger sister.

Wolborski, Stefa – Older daughter of Asta and Heniek, b. 1925.

Wolborski, Lilka – Younger daughter of Asta and Heniek, b. 1932.

SOME SURVIVORS MENTIONED IN THESE PAGES

Aksztajn, Lolek – Seen in Israel in 1970.

Gertler, David – Chief of the Sonderkommando in the ghetto. Died in Germany in the 1980s.

Husyd (probably a nickname), Moishe – Died in Germany in the early 1980s according to some survivors.

Rusek, Maniek – b. circa 1925. Survived Auschwitz, then lived in Israel.

Rusek, Michal – b. circa 1927. Survived Auschwitz, then lived in Israel.

Scheider, Cesiek – Moved from Lodz to Szczecin, his mother told me in 1964.

Weinberg – Engineer of the Lodz Ghetto Electro-technical Workshop. Lived in Lodz in 1945.

Weinberg, Jerzyk – His son. Lived in Lodz in the summer of 1945.

About the Author

Mietek Weintraub was born an only child in Lodz, Poland, on November 13, 1926, to a prosperous middle class family. He attended the Itzhak Katznelson Academy, yet was forced to stop his education in September 1939 to live in the Lodz Ghetto. After losing his father to starvation in 1941, he was sent to Auschwitz in 1944 where he was subsequently separated from his mother and where he spent one horrible week. Liberated by the American Army in Austria near the Mauthausen concentration camp in May 1945, he soon returned to Lodz in search of surviving relatives. Finding none, he traveled to Germany from where he immigrated to the USA in 1948.

He worked as a cloth cutter in various factories while attending college and graduated from the Wright Junior College in Chicago, in 1959, with an Associate in Arts Degree. He then attended Roosevelt University in Chicago, from which he graduated in 1961 with a Bachelor of Arts Degree, and went on to study at the University of Chicago, from which he graduated in 1963 with a Master of Arts Degree.

He started his teaching career as an instructor at the Purdue University in 1963 where he taught German and Russian. From 1968 until 1972, he taught Russian at the University of Kentucky, then married an Israeli and went with her to Israel where he taught English in Haifa for two years until 1974. He returned with his family to the USA in 1974 and worked as a bilingual teacher in the Chicago Public Schools until his retirement in 1989.

For the next several years, he worked as a court interpreter for the Cook County Circuit Courts and for the Federal Courts.

He has a daughter from his first marriage and two sons from his second one.

He has published three short stories up to date: *The New Neighbors*, (Jewish Magazine-2002); *My Grandparents' Seder*, (Family Gatherings-2003); *The Fragrance and the Stench*, (Wild Things-2008).